"*Parent-Child Art Psychotherapy* provides a practical framework for parent-child work in art therapy leaning on years of clinical experience. Drs. Regev and Snir weave case examples throughout the book and end with a plethora of art-based exercises and interventions. I believe that this book will benefit beginning and experienced art therapists alike, by deepening their knowledge of parent-child art therapy, the phenomenological Haifa model, developmental and psychoanalytical approaches to parent-child work and potential art-based interventions."

–Johanna Czamanski-Cohen ATR LPC (AZ), Lecturer, School of Creative Art Therapies, Faculty of Social Welfare and Health Sciences, University of Haifa, Israel

"Although an intensive clinical work, the study of parent-child psychotherapy within the framework of art therapy has been long neglected. In an attempt to fill this gap, this illuminating book summarizes and presents a rich crystallized conceptual model accompanied by a surging clinical literature to illustrate this subject. As such, almost all clinicians working with young children or applying art techniques will benefit from studying this book carefully."

–Limor Goldner, ATR PhD, Academic Advisor of Sagol Research and Treatment Laboratory for Children At-Risk, Head of the art therapy program, School of Creative Arts Therapies, University of Haifa, Israel

Parent-Child Art Psychotherapy

Parent-Child Art Psychotherapy presents a working model of ways to incorporate parents into a child's art therapy sessions, drawing on the relational-psychoanalytic notion of mentalization in the treatment of difficulties within childhood relationships. The model is introduced by clearly explaining the theory, the setting, the role of the therapist, and the work with the parents. In addition, the book offers a full section dedicated to practical applications of the model, replete with illustrative case studies and detailed therapeutic art-based interventions covering leadership, movement, collaborative and solitary work, and parent-child exercises. Intended for art therapists, students, parent-child psychotherapists, and other therapists interested in expanding their knowledge in the field, Regev and Snir provide a definition and conceptualization of a short-term treatment model with the potential to have comprehensive effects leading to positive change.

Dafna Regev is a qualified art therapist, researcher, and senior lecturer at the School of Creative Art Therapies and a faculty member of the Emili Sagol Creative Arts Therapies Research Center at the University of Haifa, Israel. She specializes in parent-child art psychotherapy and works in a private clinic. Her articles have been published in leading journals in the field of art therapy.

Sharon Snir is an art therapist and researcher. She is senior lecturer and head of the Art Therapy M.A. Program in Tel Hai College, Israel. One of her main research interests is joint drawings. Over the last few years, she has specialized in research and in teaching research in art therapy. Her articles have been published in leading journals in the field of art therapy.

Parent-Child Art Psychotherapy

Dafna Regev and Sharon Snir

Translated by Dalya Weisbrod

Routledge
Taylor & Francis Group

NEW YORK AND LONDON

First edition published 2018
by Routledge
711 Third Avenue, New York, NY 10017

and by Routledge
2 Park Square, Milton Park, Abingdon, Oxon, OX14 4RN

Routledge is an imprint of the Taylor & Francis Group, an informa business

© 2018 Taylor & Francis

Library of Congress Cataloguing-in-Publication Data
Names: Regev, Dafna, author. | Snir, Sharon, author.
Title: Parent-child art psychotherapy / Dafna Regev and Sharon Snir.
Description: First edition. | New York, NY : Routledge, 2018. |
    Includes bibliographical references.
Identifiers: LCCN 2017030231| ISBN 9781138731240 (hbk) |
    ISBN 9781138731264 (pbk) | ISBN 9781315189086 (ebk)
Subjects: | MESH: Art Therapy—methods | Child | Parent-Child
    Relations
Classification: LCC RC489.A7 | NLM WM 450.5.A8 |
    DDC 616.89/1656—dc23
LC record available at https://lccn.loc.gov/2017030231

ISBN: 978-1-138-73124-0 (hbk)
ISBN: 978-1-138-73126-4 (pbk)
ISBN: 978-1-315-18908-6 (ebk)

Typeset in Garamond
by Swales & Willis Ltd, Exeter, Devon, UK

Contents

List of Illustrations   ix
Preface   xi
Acknowledgments   xiii
Introduction   xiv

PART I
Fundamental Elements and Principles   1

1   Introduction to Parent-Child Art Psychotherapy   3

2   Presentation of the Study: Parent-Child Art Psychotherapy
in Israel   16

3   The Objectives of Parent-Child Art Psychotherapy   24

4   The Parent-Child Art Psychotherapy Setting   30

5   The Role of the Parent-Child Art Therapist   38

6   Working with Parents in the Parent-Child Art
Psychotherapy Framework   48

7   Unique Challenges in the Parent-Child Art Psychotherapy
Model   58

8   The Observation of Joint Paintings   64

PART II
Intervention Techniques   73

9   Leadership Exercises   75

10   Movement Exercises That Promote the Creation of
Images   84

11 Together and Alone   97

12 Family Exercises   124

13 An Encounter in the Interpersonal Space   136

    Index   152

Illustrations

Figures

9.1	Rachel, the mother, leads her daughter, Naomi	77
9.2	Naomi, the daughter, leads her mother, Rachel	78
9.3	Ron and Dorine in the chasing exercise	80
10.1	Erez and Lital create a joint squiggle drawing	86
10.2–10.5	Yael and Nofar splashing paint with syringes together	93
11.1–11.2	Yoav and Yarden create colored shapes on a black background	100
11.3	Yaakov and Shachar draw a forest together	106
11.4	Sharon and Tom create a joint collage	109
11.5–11.6	Efrat and Mor draw together using warm and cool colors	114
11.7	Leah and Ron complete a half drawing to create a whole drawing	118
11.8–11.10	Yonat and Adi draw and tell a story between two drawings	122
12.1	Eli and Nadav creating the parent and the child drawing in sections	131
12.2	Meital and Tal work with pictures from family life	134
13.1–13.2	Inbal and May working together without verbal communication	138, 140
13.3–13.4	Anat and Yael drawing with a tray and a marble	143, 144
13.5	Anat and Yael drawing with a tray and a marble: the daughter's first drawing	145
13.6	Anat and Yael drawing with a tray and a marble: the daughter's second drawing	146

13.7   Anat and Yael drawing with a tray and a
             marble: the mother's drawing   146
13.8–13.9   Yael and Eden walking in gouache paints   150

Tables

2.1   Demographic information on the therapists interviewed
       for this book   17
2.2   The semi-structured interview structure   19

Plates

1   Jonathan and Karen in an exercise in nine squares
2   Nechama and Limor draw animals in the forest together
3   Yael and Nofar splashing paint with syringes together
4   Yoav and Yarden create colored shapes on a black background
5   Asaf and Tamar connect the circles on the cardboard
6   Efrat and Mor draw together using warm and cool colors
7   Ya'ara and Shai work together on thirds of the page
8   Maha and Suheir following the outline of Suheir's body

Preface

We are delighted to present this book, which is the result of several years of hard work. The idea emerged from various lines of work we have conducted. In recent years, both of us have been involved in the conceptualization of working models for the field of art therapy. The decision to work on these conceptualizations materialized initially when we were art therapy students and later during our professional work, when we saw firsthand the important work that art therapists are doing in the field, and realized the lack of resonance in the professional literature. We believe that the art therapist community, which we are also a part of, consists of therapists who truly invest in their work, and have developed working models based on a range of therapeutic approaches targeted to different populations. However, along with their love for therapy and their connection to art, writing texts are less appealing to many art therapists, they are less interested in producing literature, and are sometimes afraid to put their ideas into writing. As a result, there is a great wealth of clinical knowledge but a lack of academic literature in the field.

The compilation of this book initially started out as a joint study that was published several years ago (Regev & Snir, 2014, 2015) to conceptualize and formulate a working model for parent-child art psychotherapy by gathering information about work in the field from therapists who specialize in this therapeutic approach.

Over the past few years, the field of parent-child art psychotherapy has gained popularity both worldwide and in Israel. Many of these therapists are struck by the way in which this type of therapy can make a difference in the lives of many children within a relatively limited period of time. Working both inside and outside of the therapy room accelerates the therapeutic process and suggests that significant change is possible to achieve. In Israel, the Ministry of Education now recognizes the benefits of working with this therapy model and currently provides a training program in parent-child art psychotherapy. Pioneering art therapists have begun working with children and their parents during school hours in both kindergartens and schools. This convinced us that there was a need for a clear written conceptualization of the model. In 2003, Lucille

Proulx wrote a book on parent-child dyad art therapy for infants and preschoolers. We believe that this book extends her line of thinking by providing a clinical documentation of work in the field.

Parent-child art psychotherapy has been a meeting point for the two of us as authors because our clinical and research work interconnects with our joint thinking in this area. Dafna currently combines her clinical work as an experienced parent-child art therapist and supervisor with research in the field, and also teaches parent-child art psychotherapy in art therapy training programs. Sharon has been researching the subject of joint paintings for many years, and also teaches in the field. In recent years, she has specifically researched the field of parent-child art psychotherapy.

We hope that our book opens many doors for art therapists who have yet to discover the parent-child art psychotherapy approach, and that it will lead to a more thorough understanding of art therapy with children and its reliance on work with parents. Currently in Israel, there is an association for parent-child psychotherapy that accredits therapists and supervisors in the field. We believe that this process of professionalization should lead to the development of an accredited art psychotherapy specialization as well.

References

Proulx, L. (2003). *Strengthening emotional ties through parent-child-dyad art therapy: Interventions with infants and preschoolers.* London: Jessica Kingsley.

Regev, D., & Snir, S. (2014). Working with parent-child art psychotherapy. *The Arts in Psychotherapy, 41*(5), 511–518.

Regev, D., & Snir, S. (2015). Objectives, interventions and challenges in parent-child art psychotherapy. *The Arts in Psychotherapy, 42*, 50–56.

Acknowledgments

We would like to thank the many people who assisted us in the preparation of this book. This book consists of the academic research that our students conducted while enrolled in the course "Parent-child art psychotherapy" at the University of Haifa. We would like to thank these students for helping us administer and carry out the interviews with therapists and supervisors and for their documentation of the parent-child interactions that feature in this book.

We would like to extend our thanks to the many art therapists who opened their studio doors and shared their knowledge with us. Some of them agreed to have their names mentioned in our book. Among them are Eyal Beeri Sher, Tamar Benzeev, Shlomit Chasid, Noa Dan, Hagar Dornai, Sivan Eyal, Tami Gavron, Nurit Gidron, Yael Cohen Greisman, Daphna Markman-Zinemanas, Bracha Moscovitz, Ayelet Navon, Amalia Sali, Liat Shamri, Galit Shapira, and Esti Zismann.

We would also like to acknowledge the late Mr. Peretz Hesse, and thank Tamar Hazut and Judith Siano, who were our teachers at the University of Haifa art therapy training program. The intervention exercises and techniques in this book are based on what we learned from them.

We benefited from the skilled assistance of Dalya Weisbrod, an art therapist and proficient translator, who was committed and dedicated in the translation of our different papers and articles. We would also like to thank our publisher, Taylor & Francis, and specifically Elizabeth Graber and Emma Starr, who guided us through the whole process.

And finally, this is also a wonderful opportunity to thank our dear families: the Snir family—Yehuda, Michal, Shira, and Nami—and Sharon's parents Gila and the late Jehuda Livne; and the Regev family—Alon, Maya, Inbal, Adi, and Shai, and Dafna's parents Edna and Michael Neuberger. Without you, we would not understand the importance of the relationship between parents and their children.

Introduction

Parent-Child Art Psychotherapy presents a working model that associates the fields of parent-child psychotherapy and art therapy. In the following chapters, we outline the core elements of this model as they emerged from our combined clinical knowledge and research. These descriptions and analyses are accompanied by research findings and clinical examples that shed light on the model.

The book is divided into two parts. Part I consists of Chapters 1–8, which are based on a combination of studies that were conducted in the field, as well as our clinical work spanning several years. The main objective of these chapters is to present the conceptualization of the therapeutic model from both a theoretical and clinical perspective. Chapter 1 presents a theoretical introduction to the field of parent-child art psychotherapy. Chapter 2 describes the research that served as the starting point for this book. Chapters 3–8 outline the fundamental elements and principles for working according to the parent-child art psychotherapy model as it is practiced in Israel today. These chapters define the goals of parent-child art psychotherapy (Chapter 3), the therapeutic setting (Chapter 4), the role of the therapist (Chapter 5), working with parents (Chapter 6), the difficulties of parent-child art psychotherapy (Chapter 7), and, finally, a guide to the observation of joint paintings (Chapter 8). Part II covers intervention techniques and variants on the joint painting technique. Chapter 9 presents a series of joint painting exercises that explore alternating and strengthening leadership roles in the parent-child dynamic. Chapter 10 introduces a series of different free, playful exercises that gradually promote the creation of a projective image that represents internal content and serves as the focus of parent-child research. Chapter 11 presents exercises that encourage the transition between being together and being separate, and enhances the ability of the dyad to shift between intimacy and autonomy within the parent-child relationship. Chapter 12 introduces methods to prompt parent and child to describe family representations according to projective techniques. Chapter 13 describes joint painting techniques that distort and blur the boundaries between the two creators, and hence compel them to act as a single unit.

Part I

Fundamental Elements and Principles

1 Introduction to Parent-Child Art Psychotherapy

History of the Parent-Child Psychotherapy Approach

In the parent-child psychotherapy approach, both parent and child are present in the therapy room together, and the therapeutic process centers on their relationship. Today, the presence of a parent in the therapy room tends to be taken for granted, but this is a relatively new therapeutic development that has made emotional therapy with very young children possible. This approach is particularly important for children and toddlers who go through enormous developmental changes while acquiring new essential skills. Therapeutic change is thought to be more feasible in early childhood precisely because this is a period of developmental change. Teachers and therapists as well as developmental and educational psychologists all concur that early intervention for young children who are experiencing emotional, social, and functioning difficulties is crucial, and that this type of psychotherapy can lead to change. This may explain why growing numbers of therapists are engaging in parent-child psychotherapy with older children as well, particularly when a specific client can benefit developmentally from this approach.

This chapter summarizes the major milestones in parent-child psychotherapy. For many years, it was believed that psychotherapy for children should be based on the same conventional therapeutic techniques used for adults. These techniques included awareness of object relations, identifications, transference, and interpersonal features. Melanie Klein (1932), who addressed the issue of psychotherapy with children, and Anna Freud (1928) both believed that children could not be given the same treatment as adults because the child's ego is not sufficiently developed, objects have not yet been fully internalized, and their awareness and realistic view of the world are limited (Stern, 2005). Gradually, techniques have been developed that consider and relate to children's processes of emotional development, while recognizing their abilities and play activities as crucial therapeutic factors for emotional health (Albon, 2001).

Over the years, the systemic approach has become increasingly recognized. The field of emotional therapy now relies less on intrapsychic psychology, and more on intersubjective psychology, while emphasizing the importance of interpersonal relationships as a key element in the development of emotional well-being (Aron, 2013). The prevailing therapeutic approaches for children were heavily criticized for their lack of attention to the concrete family in the therapy room. Their absence hindered the disclosure of important information about family relationships and communication and the possibility of creating change (e.g., Minuchin, 2007). Child psychotherapy gained ground when initial studies showed that the family unit is crucial to the child and must be addressed during the observation and therapeutic process (Bateson, Jackson, Haley, & Weakland, 1956; Bowen, 1959). The importance of the parent-child relationship to child development and well-being has been emphasized by various theorists (Bowlby, 1979; Klein, 1975; Mahler, Pine, & Bergman, 1975; Stern, 1995; Winnicott, 1971). Together, they all attribute considerable significance to the relationship between the child and the parents in general, and in particular the relationship with the mother. Object relations theory posits that the building blocks of an individual's personality, development, and mental health are closely linked to the infant's relationships with both the caregiving figure and parents (Klein, 1975; Mahler et al., 1975; Winnicott, 1971). It is argued that patterns of attachment with the mother figure influence the child's self-perception and perception of others, and thus shape the child's future relationships with others (Bowlby, 1979; Bretherton, 1990; Stern, 2004; Winnicott, 1971). In recent decades, a new school of research and clinical work has emerged that aims to develop innovative therapeutic models that incorporate the parent into the therapeutic process. These include family therapy and parent-child psychotherapy, which both relate to the needs of the parents as well.

Parent-child psychotherapy is a psychodynamic approach derived from the intersubjective school that views the individual as developing and growing within and through relationships with others. This approach is based on object relations theory, which deals with the early growth of the self in relationships with others (Segal, 1977; Winnicott, 1971), as well as Bowlby's attachment theory (Bretherton, 1992). It focuses on sub-family relationships to treat disorders in relationships in the pre-latency period (Stern, 2005). Whereas individual therapy often makes an analogy between the parent-child and the therapist-client relationship (Fonagy & Target, 1998), in parent-child psychotherapy, the focus shifts from transferred relationships from the past to processing the object relations in the present (Kaplan, Harel, & Avimeir-Patt, 2010). There are many parent-child psychotherapy approaches, each with a slightly different emphasis on the role of the therapist. However, all their therapeutic goals have to do with the relationship between parent and child (Harel, Kaplan, Avimeir-Patt, & Ben-Aaron, 2006; Kaplan et al., 2010; Lieberman, 2004; McDonough, 2000; Muir, 1992). All forms of parent-child psychotherapy require at least one parent, and from time to time both parents, in the therapy room.

The Haifa Parent-Child Psychotherapy Model

Most therapists in Israel who work according to the parent-child approach have adopted the Haifa model, which was developed by the late Miriam Ben-Aaron and colleagues (Ben-Aaron, Harel, Kaplan, & Patt, 2001; Harel et al., 2006; Kaplan et al., 2010). The Haifa model is based on the concept of mentalization, as defined by the psychoanalytic-relational school (Fonagy, Steele, Moran, Steele, & Higgit, 1991; Fonagy & Target, 1997; Fonagy, Gergely, & Target, 2007) to treat difficulties in childhood relationships. The key concepts of the Haifa model are explained in detail below.

Internal Representations

Object relations theory posits that the numerous interactions that individuals experience during their lifetime with significant others are stored as abstract representations in memory (Stern, 1985). These representations, which are a composite of countless interactions, contain information about who the person is in the relationship (self-representation). For example, am I of value? Am I worthy of love? Am I competent? They contain general information about other people and what characterizes them (representation of other). For example, can I rely on others? Do they have the strength to change things? Are they empathetic toward me? Internal representations are used as a script or scenario on which to base expectations of relationships with others, and also include information about relationships, and the routes and strategies to achieve intimacy and love, as well as independence and autonomy (Bretherton, 2005; Bretherton & Munholland, 2008). People differ in their representations of their relationships because they have different relational histories. Some have learned that the best way to get close to their mothers is to call out and express a need for her presence. Other individuals have learned that their mother will only respond after they have cried for a long period of time. Yet others know that their mother will only let them stay close if they are quiet and do not bother her with their problems, distress, or wishes. All this information is stored in what is referred to as the "internal representations" by object relations theory.

Throughout our lives and as a function of our experiences, we develop a hierarchy of representations that distinguish between types of relationships. During a new interaction, we elicit the appropriate representation to know what we can expect from ourselves, from others and from the relationship with others, and also to identify the best course of action to take in order to achieve our objectives. One of the representations that we develop during our lives is the parental representation. Parental representations are representations in memory of conscious and unconscious content that include perceptions, fantasies, hopes, fears, and expectations

(Araneda, Santelices, & Farkas, 2010; Ilicali & Fisek, 2004) regarding parental roles. These include information about the relationship of the parent with the child, the way parents perceive themselves in their parental role, and the way they perceive their child (Slade & Cohen, 1996). Parental representations are created through early memories of the experiences of the relationship that parents had with their primary caregivers, and are the result of the parents' internalization, organizing, and acceptance of the relationship with and treatment by their parents or alternative primary caregivers (Dayton, Levendosky, Davidson, & Bogat, 2010).

Internal representations are typically hidden and concealed (Fonagy, 2001), and we often activate them without realizing it. During an interaction between a child and parent in parent-child psychotherapy, these representations are activated and become rekindled in a way that allows for observation and mental processing. The child activates the developing representation of the relationship with his or her parents and with others, and the parent activates the parental representations that emerge during interactions with their child. These representations are heavily influenced by the parents' past experiences, and they affect the way the parent responds to the child. Thus, in the clinic, parents are often affected by their parental representations to such an extent that it makes it difficult for them to see their actual child, and hinders their ability to adequately tend to their child's unique need for support (Kaplan et al., 2010). For example, a mother who had a very symbiotic relationship with her mother for many years may have problems acknowledging that she is recreating a similar relationship with her daughter. The parent-child psychotherapist plays an important role when working with these representations. For this reason, Kaplan et al. (2010) defined the goal of parent-child psychotherapy as follows:

> The goal is to encourage changes in the experiences of the parent and the child, as well as in their characteristic patterns of interaction that are based on the existing representations. The changes in these interactions lead to changes in representations, and therefore the goal is twofold, changing both the actual behavior, as well as the representation of the self, the other and the relationship. (p. 34)

Mentalization

Another key concept underlying parent-child psychotherapy is "mentalization." Fonagy and colleagues (Fonagy et al., 1991) defined mentalization, or the reflective function, as the ability to understand the behavior of the self and others in terms of mental states (thoughts, feelings, beliefs, desires, and strategies). In practice, mentalization connects cognitive and emotional components to know the self and others. The reflective function develops within a secure relationship, when the parents help their children think about experiences, and this teaches the children to understand their individual emotions. For example, many parents are familiar with the situation in which a child does not go to bed on time (let's assume due to a family event). The child becomes irritable, angry, and whiny in an atypical manner. The reflective ability of the parent to understand the child's experience and predicament, and in view of the undesirable behavior, helps the parent direct the child in a way that can resolve the problem (e.g., speeding up the ritual, and by starting the process earlier in the future). This helps the child understand his or her inner feelings: "I am not a bad child, or a problematic child. I am a tired child." As part of development, children acquire an understanding about mentalization processes from their parents. However, occasionally the child experiences a difficulty, or the parent responds to the child via parental representations, or there are communication problems. In these circumstances, the parent may not be able to activate reflective thinking to understand the reason for the child's behavior (the parent may feel overwhelmed or identify with the behavior). In such cases, this ability is blocked. For example, a parent who suffered extreme social rejection during childhood and could have a self-representation of an individual of no value as a result, may lack the ability to make connections, and hence view the outside world as isolated. This parent will find it hard to help his or her child to understand experiences and cope with them, particularly when the child experiences rejection. In such a case, the child may have trouble understanding how to cope with a situation and struggle to mentalize and think of the self and others in different contexts.

In parent-child psychotherapy, mentalization serves as both the goal and the method behind the therapeutic process. The aim is to reach a state in which both the parent and the child (depending on the age and stage of development) are capable of being involved in the process of mentalization, and understand the actions and motivations of the parent-child relationship. The therapist helps the parent and the child through this learning curve by engaging in and practicing reflective abilities during therapy sessions (Kaplan et al., 2010). For instance, in the example above, once the parent is able to engage in a mentalization process of the rejection experienced during childhood while participating in parental training, he or she may gradually become more attentive and available to the child and think reflectively together about social events that the child has experienced.

The Haifa Parent-Child Psychotherapy Model in Clinical Practice

Self-representation and mentalization are crucial features of the Haifa parent-child psychotherapy model. This model acknowledges the complexity of parenting and the processes of change that parents often experience

(Cohen, 2007). It helps gain a deeper understanding of the dynamics of intergenerational transference of psycho-pathological parental representations and ways to prevent such processes. The intergenerational transference of patterns of behavior, including neglect and abuse and the prevention of such behaviors, are built into the model through the concepts of attachment, maternal sensitivity, mentalization, and the ability to self-regulate (Fonagy, Gergely, Jurist, & Target, 2002). The model assumes that children develop a unique relationship with each parent, and that they need the active participation of both parents in their lives (Kaplan et al., 2010). When working within this model, the therapeutic setting includes weekly meetings with the same therapist and alternating mother-child and father-child sessions. Every two or three weeks, the therapist meets with both parents without the child for parent training purposes. During the sessions when the child is present, the therapist can observe how the main themes that characterize the parent-child relationship are recreated in the therapy room. Through play and dialogue, children often show parents how they need their support. The parents and child work to build new patterns in the relationship and create new meanings for their behavior. One of the most important aims in therapy is the differentiation between the child and the parents. Here, the therapist's role is to help clarify the distinction between the child's needs and wishes, and those of the parents. During the parent training sessions, the therapist focuses the conversation on the child. The therapist and parents discuss what took place in each parent-child session. The main issue addressed during parent training is the parental representations that impact the child, and the main objective is to help the parents help their children (Kaplan et al., 2010).

The Implementation of the Parent-Child Art Psychotherapy Model

This section addresses the implementation of the Haifa parent-child psychotherapy model in art therapy.

Art Therapy

Art therapy is a method of emotional therapy that is nonverbal and involves processing conscious and unconscious content reflected in a creative process. This therapeutic field was defined by the American Art Therapy Association (AATA) as follows:

> Art therapy is a mental health profession in which clients, facilitated by the art therapist, use art media, the creative process, and the resulting artwork to explore their feelings, reconcile emotional conflicts, foster self-awareness, manage behavior and addictions, develop social skills, improve reality orientation, reduce anxiety, and increase self-esteem. (American Art Therapy Association, 2016)

As part of art therapy, the art materials, the creative process, and the creative product itself all serve as means of self-inquiry, self-expression, and a way to develop insights and create change (Case & Dalley, 2006; Malchiodi, 2011). Art therapy's uniqueness stems from the use of art as a language. It enables nonverbal indirect dialogue that helps bypass defenses and allows individuals to express themselves, particularly those who are unable to articulate by themselves or have difficulty with verbal communication for various reasons (Karkou & Glasman, 2004). The visual product created during art therapy is considered to reflect the cognitive, emotional, and communicative aspects of the creator's personality. The visual product is also an organized and tangible expression of abstract emotional and mental content (Markman-Zinemanas, 2013). Feelings, fantasies, and thoughts are transferred from mental experiences and appear as visual and realistic phenomena in the artwork (Betensky, 1995). Numerous approaches concur that art allows for the expression of nonverbal internal representations. During the artistic process, the creator's representations of the past are composed and reflected in an art form through the use of images and symbols (Robbins, 2001).

Over the years, a variety of art therapy approaches have developed to cope with a wide range of difficulties. Although there are many differences across approaches, art materials play an important role in all of them, and are the building blocks for verbal communication in the therapeutic process. The dialogue created through the use of art materials bridges to internal experiences, and thus constitutes a point of encounter between the creator and the therapist, and the creator and him or herself (Sotto, 2008).

A key element in the therapeutic process is the process of evaluation, which, unlike diagnostic assessments that include distinct indicators, aims to extend and develop the observation of the artwork and achieve a broader understanding of the client. The rationale for continuous evaluation emerges from the need to collect information about clients' states of mind, the issues that the clients are dealing with, their needs, their difficulties, their abilities, their responses to therapy, and the extent to which the therapy is suitable for them. These are common to all art therapy approaches (Gussak & Rosal, 2016), including parent-child art psychotherapy. Although the objectives and methods of evaluation differ across approaches, observing the artwork and the creative process, and striving to understand the content conveyed during the creative process all play an important role in therapy, and are crucial windows for art therapists.

Parent-Child Art Psychotherapy

The parent-child art psychotherapy model used primarily in Israel is a combination of the Haifa parent-child psychotherapy model and art therapy. In this model, both the creative process and the art product are central elements to therapy that encourage the production of crucial mental processes (Gavron, 2010). The model provides parent and child with a visual artistic experience that uses the imagination, and allows for nonverbal symbolic expression during an artistic activity that both the adult and child do together (Proulx, 2003). A unique feature of parent-child art psychotherapy is the range of art materials and artistic techniques made available by the therapist as a function of the child's developmental stage, which also allows parents to create art in a way that is appropriate on both a symbolic and psychological level for them as well. Often, the tangible encounter between parents and their artwork allows them to translate significant conscious and unconscious content into words (Gavron, 2010). The incorporation of artistic creation into the therapeutic process fulfills the two goals of the Haifa parent-child psychotherapy model: the creation of an interpersonal interaction as a space for change, and the provision for parent and child to observe and examine their internal representations.

The Creation of an Interpersonal Interaction as a Space for Change

Clinicians report that when parent and child use art materials and create an artwork, a powerful form of communication and interpersonal interaction emerges. The art therapist's role is to show how to use the materials or to provide technical assistance (Gottlieb, 1999). Working with art materials encourages playfulness, creativity, and self-expression (Moon, 2010). At times, the parent-child interaction takes the form of the creation of a joint artwork (Markman-Zinemanas & Gvuli-Margalit, 2003). The interactions surrounding the artwork enable therapeutic intervention at a behavioral level of the relationship, and strengthen the bond between parent and child (Proulx, 2003).

Offering the Parent and the Child an Opportunity to Observe Internal Representations of the Relationship

While the parent and child interact in the therapy room through artwork, the internal representations of the self, the other, and the relationship between them are reflected symbolically. This symbolic reflection emerges from the creative process and by working with the materials, which includes one's attitude toward the materials, the page, and the other. The creative product serves as a projective space for these internal representations (Gavron, 2010). Observing the artistic creation and recalling the creative process allows for further acknowledgment and processing of the representations that were expressed (Markman-Zinemanas, 2011). At times, working with art materials as part of the therapeutic process can be free and open, whereas at others there are attempts to structure the process. One example of a more structured session can be seen in the work of Tami Gavron, who has developed an assessment tool for evaluating parent-child relationships using art (Gavron, 2010, 2013; Gavron & Mayseless, 2015).

There is some support for the assumption that representations of the mother-child relationship will surface and affect the interaction during the creation of joint artwork. Bar-On (2014) and Regev and Patishi (2017) examined the connection between maternal representations and the responses of 80 mothers to their joint paintings with their children aged 5–7. They found that positive representations of the child and the relationship as warm and close were linked to a more positive perception of the process of creating the joint painting, as well as viewing the experience as more enjoyable, profound, meaningful, flowing, pleasant, and positive. Similarly, negative aspects of the mother's perception of her responses to the joint painting were shown to be related to her perception of the situation. Mothers who felt a sense of coldness, alienation, and rejection in the relationship with their child and perceived the relationship as a locus of conflict tended to view the joint painting with their child as less profound and meaningful, as well as less flowing, positive, and essential.

Chasid (2016), who compared a parent-child art psychotherapy group with an art therapy group where the mothers were not present, found support for the assumption that parent-child art psychotherapy can lead to a change in maternal representations. Chasid found that compared to the mothers of children who participated in the art therapy group, mothers in the parent-child art psychotherapy group showed an improvement in their perceptions of their relationships with their children, their perceptions of the quality of the communication with their children, and a decrease in feelings of alienation and rejection. The mothers also viewed their relationships with their children as closer. Similarly, Shapira, Lev-Wiezel, and Raz (2014), who interviewed mothers who participated in parent-child art psychotherapy, found that after therapy, the mothers viewed their relationships with their children as depending heavily on their ability to understand the inner world of their child and their ability as mothers to allow for separation within the relationship. This also extends to the importance of having interpersonal communication, a close relationship, and the regulation of intimacy and emotions between the parent and child. The characteristics of this change included the mother's ability to understand the child's inner world, allow for separation and appropriate communication, understand the child's need for closeness, and regulate the relationship. Several other studies (e.g., Hosea, 2006; Plante & Berneche, 2008; Ponteri, 2001) have provided initial support for the idea that one of the outcomes of parent-child art psychotherapy is that mothers reported more positive representations of the mother-child relationship.

Thus, overall, although the combined use of parent-child psychotherapy and art therapy is recent and still developing, it is attracting growing numbers of art therapists who are now learning to use this approach successfully. In the following chapters, we outline the core elements of this model, as they emerged from our research and our combined clinical knowledge.

Summary

- Parent-child art psychotherapy is based on the idea that the parent-child relationship is a key component of the child's welfare. For this reason, this relationship forms the core of therapy with children.
- The parent-child art psychotherapy model is based on the idea that art is a vehicle for creating meaningful interactions between parent and child.
- The incorporation of art-making into the therapeutic process helps to achieve the two goals of therapy defined by the Haifa parent-child psychotherapy model: the creation of interpersonal interaction as a space for change, and giving parent and child the opportunity to observe and examine their internal representations through artwork.

References

Albon, L. S. (2001). The work of transformation: Changes in technique since Anna Freud's normality and pathology in childhood. *The Psychoanalytic Study of the Child, 56*, 27–38.

American Art Therapy Association (2016). *About art therapy*. Retrieved from http://arttherapy.org/.

Araneda, M. E., Santelices, M. P., & Farkas, C. (2010). Building infant-mother attachment: The relationship between attachment style, socio-emotional well-being and maternal representations. *Journal of Reproductive and Infant Psychology, 28*(1), 30–43.

Aron, L. (2013). *A meeting of minds: Mutuality in psychoanalysis* (Vol. 4). New York, NY: Routledge.

Bar-On, J. (2014). *Mothers' perception of her parenting and her reaction to a joint painting with her child*. (Unpublished Master's Dissertation). University of Haifa, Israel. (In Hebrew).

Bateson, G., Jackson, D. D., Haley, J., & Weakland, J. H. (1956). Towards a theory of schizophrenia. *Behavioral Science, 1*, 251–264.

Ben-Aaron, M., Harel, J., Kaplan, H., & Patt, R. (2001). *Mother-child and father-child psychotherapy: A manual for the treatment of relational disturbances in childhood*. London and Philadelphia, PA: Whurr.

Betensky, M. (1995). *What do you see? Phenomenology of therapeutic art expression*. London: Jessica Kingsley.

Bowen, M. (1959). Family relationship in schizophrenia. In A. Auerbach (Ed.), *Schizophrenia: An integrated approach* (pp. 147–178). New York, NY: Ronald.

Bowlby, J. (1979). *The making and breaking of affectional bonds*. London: Tavistock.

Bretherton, I. (1990). Communication patterns, internal working models, and the intergenerational transmission of attachment relationships. *Infant Mental Health Journal, 11*, 237–252.

Bretherton, I. (1992). The origins of attachment theory: John Bowlby and Mary Ainsworth. *Developmental Psychology, 28*, 759–775.

Bretherton, I. (2005). In pursuit of the internal working model construct and its relevance to attachment relationships. In K. E. Grossmann, K. Grossmann, & E. Waters (Eds.), *Attachment from infancy to adulthood: The major longitudinal studies* (pp. 13–47). New York, NY: Guilford Press.

Bretherton I., & Munholland, K. A. (2008). Internal working models in attachment relationships: Elaborating a central construct in attachment theory. In J. Cassidy & P. R. Shaver (Eds.), *Handbook of attachment second edition: Theory, research, and clinical applications* (pp. 102–130). New York, NY: Guilford Press.

Case, C., & Dalley, T. (2006). *The handbook of art therapy*. New York, NY: Routledge.

Chasid, S. (2016). *The effectiveness of group parent-child art psychotherapy.* (Unpublished Master's Dissertation). University of Haifa, Israel. (In Hebrew).

Cohen, A. (2007). *Becoming a parent: Relationships, challenges and development*. Kiryat Bialik: Ach Publishing. (In Hebrew).

Dayton, C. J., Levendosky, A. A., Davidson, W. S., & Bogat, G. A. (2010). The child as held in the mind of the mother: The influence of parental maternal representations on parenting behaviors. *Infant Mental Health Journal, 31*, 220–241.

Fonagy, P. (2001). Changing ideas of change: The dual components of therapeutic action. In J. Edwards (Ed.), *Being alive: Building on the work of Anne Alvarez* (pp. 14–31). London: Brunner-Routledge.

Fonagy, P., Gergely, G., Jurist, E. L., & Target, M. (2002). *Affect regulation, mentalization and the development of the self*. New York, NY: Other Press.

Fonagy, P., Gergely, G., & Target, M. (2007). The parent–infant dyad and the construction of the subjective self. *Journal of Child Psychology and Psychiatry, 48*(3/4), 288–328.

Fonagy, P., Steele, H., Moran, G., Steele, M., & Higgit, A. (1991). The capacity for understanding mental states: The reflective self in parent and child and its significance for security of attachment. *Infant Mental Health Journal, 12*(3), 201–218.

Fonagy, P., & Target, M. (1997). Attachment and reflective function: Their role in self organization. *Development and Psychopathology, 9*, 679–900.

Fonagy, P., & Target, M. (1998). An interpersonal view of the infant. In A. Hurry (Ed.), *Psychoanalysis and developmental therapy* (pp. 3–31). London: Karnac Books.

Freud, A. (1928). *Introduction to the technique of child analysis* (L. P. Clark, trans.). New York: Nervous and Mental Disease Publishing.

Gavron, T. (2010). Assessment and parent-child art psychotherapy. In H. Kaplan, J. Harel, & R. Avimeir-Patt (Eds.), *Parent-child therapy: The therapeutic encounter between theory and practice* (pp. 390–414). Haifa: University of Haifa. (In Hebrew).

Gavron, T. (2013). Meeting on common ground: Assessing parent-child relationships through the joint painting procedure. *Art Therapy: Journal of the American Art Therapy Association, 30*(1), 12–19.

Gavron, T., & Mayseless, O. (2015). The joint painting procedure to assess implicit aspects of the mother-child relationship in middle childhood. *Art Therapy: Journal of the American Art Therapy Association, 32*(2), 83–88.

Gottlieb, T. (1999). Some aspects of art therapy: Working with children and youth. *Issues in Special Education and Rehabilitation, 14*(1), 65–73. (In Hebrew).

Gussak, D. E., & Rosal, M. L. (Eds.). (2016). *The Wiley handbook of art therapy*. Oxford: John Wiley & Sons.

Harel, J., Kaplan, H., Avimeir-Patt, R., & Ben-Aaron, M. (2006). The child's active role in mother-child, father-child psychotherapy: A psychodynamic approach to the treatment of relational disturbances. *Psychology and Psychotherapy: Theory, Research and Practice, 79*(1), 23–36.

Hosea, H. (2006). "The brush's footmarks": Parents and infants paint together in a small community art therapy group. *International Journal of Art Therapy, 11*(2), 69–78.

Ilicali, E. T., & Fisek, G. O. (2004). Maternal representations during pregnancy and early motherhood. *Infant Mental Health Journal, 26*, 16–27.

Kaplan, H., Harel, Y., & Avimeir-Patt, R. (2010). *Parent-child psychotherapy: An encounter between the therapeutic act and theory*. Department of Psychology, University of Haifa. (In Hebrew).

Karkou, V., & Glasman, J. (2004). Arts, education and society: The role of the arts in promoting the emotional wellbeing and social inclusion of young people. *Support for Learning, 19*(2), 57–65.

Klein, M. (1932). *The psycho-analysis of children*. London: The Hogarth Press.

Klein, M. (1975). *Love, guilt and reparation & other works, 1921–1945*. New York, NY: Delacorte Press.

Lieberman, A. F. (2004). Child-parent psychotherapy: A relationship-based approach to the treatment of mental health disorders in infancy and early childhood. In A. J. Sameroff, S. C. McDonough, & K. L. Rosenblum (Eds.), *Treating parent-infant relationship problems* (pp. 97–122). New York, NY: Guilford Press.

Mahler, M. S., Pine, F., & Bergman, A. (1975). *The psychological birth of the human infant*. New York, NY: Basic Books.

Malchiodi, C. A. (Ed.). (2011). *Handbook of art therapy*. New York, NY: Guilford Press.

Markman-Zinemanas, D. (2011). The additional value of art psychotherapy: Visual symbolization. *Academic Journal of Creative Art Therapies, 2*, 131–139.

Markman-Zinemanas, D. (2013). *When the implicit becomes explicit: Art psychotherapy*. Tel Aviv: Resling.

Markman-Zinemanas, D., & Gvuli-Margalit, V. (2003). Interaction in art projects as a major tool in the therapeutic process. Presented at: *The International Conference of Art Therapy*, Budapest.

McDonough, S. C. (2000). Interaction guidance: An approach for difficult to engage families. In C. Zeanah (Ed.), *Handbook of infant mental health* (pp. 485–493). New York, NY: Guildford Press.

Minuchin, S. (2007). Forty years of family therapy. In D. Gilad (Ed.), *Lecture at a conference of the Israel Association for Family and Couple Therapy*. Ramat Efal. (In Hebrew).

Moon, C. (2010). *Materials and media in art therapy: Critical understandings of diverse artistic vocabularies*. New York, NY: Routledge.

Muir, E. (1992). Watching, waiting and wondering: Applying psychoanalytic principles to mother-infant intervention. *Infant Mental Health Journal, 13*(4), 319–328.

Plante, P., & Berneche, R. (2008). A phenomenological study addressing the reinforcement of emotional ties between parent and child through the elaboration and evaluation of dyadic art therapy groups. *Canadian Art Therapy Association Journal, 21,* 18–34.

Ponteri, A. K. (2001). The effect of group art therapy on depressed mothers and their children. *Art Therapy: Journal of the American Art Therapy Association, 18*(3), 148–157.

Proulx, L. (2003). *Strengthening emotional ties through parent-child-dyad art therapy: Interventions with infants and preschoolers.* London: Jessica Kingsley.

Regev, D., & Patishi, R. (2017). Mothers' perceptions of their relationships with their children and their responses to joint drawings. *International Journal of Art Therapy, 1–7.*

Robbins, A. (2001). Object relations and art therapy. In J. A. Rubin (Ed.), *Approaches to art therapy: Theory and technique* (pp. 54–65). Philadelphia, PA: Brunner-Routledge.

Segal, H. (1977). *The work of Hanna Segal: A Kleinian approach to clinical practice.* Northvale, NJ: Jason Aronson.

Shapira, G., Lev-Wiezel, R., & Raz, A. (2014). Mothers' perceptions of their relationship with their children following dyadic art therapy. *The International Journal of Social Sciences and Humanities Invention, 1*(5), 369–397.

Slade, A., & Cohen, L. (1996). The process of parenting and the remembrance of things past. *Infant Mental Health Journal, 17,* 217–238.

Sotto, L. (2008). *Being in touch.* Haifa: Pardes. (In Hebrew).

Stern, D. N. (1985). *The interpersonal world of the infant: A view from psychoanalysis and developmental psychology.* New York, NY: Basic Books.

Stern, D. N. (1995). *The motherhood constellation.* New York, NY: Basic Books.

Stern, D. N. (2004). *The present moment in psychotherapy and everyday life.* New York, NY and London: Norton.

Stern, E. (2005). *Post-therapy outcome check between Ben-Aaron's parent-child psychotherapy and individual therapy patients.* (Unpublished Master's Dissertation). University of Haifa, Israel. (In Hebrew).

Winnicott, D. W. (1971). *Playing and reality.* London: Tavistock.

2 Presentation of the Study

Parent-Child Art Psychotherapy in Israel

The field of art therapy is still in its initial stages of development as an academic discipline. As with other subjects in this field, it seems to be the case that clinicians accumulate knowledge and know-how, and this information is then transmitted verbally from supervisors to therapists who work in the field. When we were art therapy students, we often asked why this vast repository of practical knowledge and skills had not been systematically recorded and collected to form a working model that we could draw on as therapists for therapeutic purposes. As teachers, we realized how important this issue was when we became engaged in training future art therapists. We then found ourselves searching for theoretical and empirical articles and educational material that described work in the field more thoroughly and inclusively. This prompted us to approach experts in parent-child art psychotherapy to document and collect the knowledge that they possessed in the field, including the goals of therapy, the therapeutic setting, therapeutic interventions, the characteristics of working with parents, and the difficulties experienced along the way. This book addresses these topics and attempts to shed light on the key components of parent-child art psychotherapy as it is currently practiced in Israel. It describes therapeutic work in the field as implemented by a relatively large number of therapists. We aim to link theory and practice in a way that will assist therapists in the field, as well as art therapy students in their training.[1]

This chapter outlines how we conducted this study, and the principles of parent-child art psychotherapy in Israel. The next chapters expand on these principles and provide clinical examples.

The Participants

To gather information on the principles of parent-child art therapy in Israel, we interviewed 20 parent-child art therapists (19 women and 1 man), ranging in age from 36 to 61 (see Table 2.1). In the first stage, 15 parent-child therapists were approached and agreed to participate in

Table 2.1 Demographic information on the therapists interviewed for this book

Therapist number	Age	Gender	Theoretical orientation	Practical supervision	Workplace	Seniority and years working as a parent–child therapist
1	42	Female	Psychodynamic, phenomenological, and narrative	Yes	Private and public	5
2	59	Female	Eclectic	Yes	Public	6
3	48	Female	Object relations and attachment	Yes	Private and public	5
4	53	Female	Psychodynamic and phenomenological	Yes	Private	26
5	39	Female	Psychoanalytical and object relations	Yes	Private and public	5
6	43	Female	Eclectic	Yes	Private	12
7	41	Female	Psychodynamic, object relations, and family therapy	Yes	Private and public	4
8	50	Female	Psychoanalytical and relational	Yes	Private	17
9	40	Female	Psychodynamic	Yes	Private and public	10
10	40	Female	Psychodynamic and object relations	Yes	Private	10
11	36	Female	Eclectic, emphasis on psychoanalytic	No	Public	1
12	51	Female	Psychoanalytic	Yes	Public	6
13	56	Female	Adlerian and cognitive behavioral	No	Private and public	5
14	61	Female	Developmental, relational, and object relations	Yes	Private	18
15	55	Female	Psychodynamic and phenomenological	Yes	Private and public	12
16	55	Female	Psychodynamic and phenomenological	Yes	Private	15
17	54	Male	Object relations and self-psychology	No	Private and public	4
18	55	Female	Psychodynamic and object relations	Yes	Private and public	15
19	50	Female	Eclectic, emphasis on psychoanalytic	Yes	Private and public	8
20	42	Female	Object relations	No	Public	5

semi-structured interviews. Eleven of the therapists who were interviewed during the first stage and five additional therapists took part in the subsequent feedback stage.

All the participants, who are experts in the field of parent-child art psychotherapy, were invited to take part in the research using the snowball sampling method, where participants recommend their peers who are thought to be suitable candidates. All the participants work at accredited institutions. All the art therapists who took part in the interview stage agreed to the terms that the interviews would be used for research purposes only and each signed a consent form. In order to protect the identity of the clients discussed by these therapists, all names have been changed, and the examples in the interviews have no identifying information.

Methodology

The interviews with the therapists were semi-structured to allow the participants to express their perceptions of their work in a detailed manner, and describe and illustrate their work with examples from their therapeutic practice (McCracken, 1988). The interview guidelines included the following primary content areas: the place of parent-child psychotherapy in the therapist's professional life, the type of population with whom the therapist works, the therapy setting, the therapeutic contract with clients, the goals of therapy, the extent to which the therapist uses assessments or diagnostic evaluation techniques through art, types of interventions used by the therapist, the perception of the role of the therapist, the presence and the significance of art in the therapy room, the process of parent training, the success or failure of parent-child psychotherapy, difficulties in therapy, and the influence of the therapist as a parent during therapy sessions. Each of these questions was presented to the participants as the interview progressed. In addition, a number of supplementary questions were prepared within each content area, which could be used to gain a deeper understanding during the interviews in the event that the answer to the main question was insufficient. These are summarized in Table 2.2.

Data Collection

Initially, art therapy graduate students at the University of Haifa who were enrolled in Dafna's "Parent-child art psychotherapy" course approached potential participants. These students were trained to carry out the interviews. One of the students contacted participants by phone, explained the purpose of the study, and asked for their verbal consent to take part. All 15 therapists who were approached agreed to give interviews. Interviews lasted between one and two hours and were held at the convenience of the therapist in public clinics, public spaces, or in the therapist's home.

Table 2.2 The semi-structured interview structure

Primary questions	Supplementary questions
Please tell me about yourself.	Where do you work? Where did you study? How many years have you worked in the field? When did you start parent-child art psychotherapy? How did you get into this field? Please elaborate on the events/experiences in your life that led you to choose the field of parent-child art psychotherapy. What parent-child approach do you use?
Please tell me about the importance of parent-child art psychotherapy in your professional life today.	Do you work exclusively as a parent-child therapist? If not, within your therapeutic work, how much of your work is allocated to parent-child art psychotherapy? How do you feel about this kind of work? (Do you like it? Do you believe in its strengths?) What do you like about this model? What is your connection to the field?
Which populations do you work with?	What are the typical age groups? Do families approach you on their own or are they referred to you by anyone? What types of difficulties or problems do you view as appropriate for this model? Which populations/difficulties do you personally prefer to work with? How do you view this preference? Is there a population you would not treat in parent-child art psychotherapy?

(continued)

Table 2.2 (continued)

Primary questions	Supplementary questions
What does the therapeutic setting look like?	What does the therapy room look like? Is there something you would like to change? What is the difference between a clinic that is specifically for parent–child art psychotherapy and a clinic for individual art therapy? What is in the therapy room? What is the structure and the frequency of the sessions, who is present, and how many times do you meet? What is the length of a session? Do you work with one parent–child dyad at a time, or in groups? Do the sessions have a fixed structure? If so, what?
What is the therapeutic contract with the clients?	What are the ground rules that are defined at the beginning of the therapeutic process with the parents? With the child and the parents? Are there any general rules in the therapy room? Is there anything that you would not allow the children/parents to do in the room? What are your limits?
What are the general goals of therapy?	
Do you use any assessments or evaluation techniques through art? If yes, which ones, and how do you analyze the findings?	
What types of interventions do you implement in the therapy room?	
What is your role as a therapist?	Do you try to serve as a role model? Do you interfere in the interactions between parents and child? To what extent and where are you active in the therapy room? Do you speak with the parents on behalf of the child? Do you give parents advice? Do you give parents any psychological-educational information? How do you relate to the many levels of transference that take place in the therapy room?

Tell me about the presence of art in the therapy room.	What materials do you offer to your clients?
	Are there specific materials that you do not use during parent-child art psychotherapy?
	How does art contribute to therapy? What does art promote that is different from play?
	How much time does the art activity take during the session?
	Do you allow for free creative work, or do you guide parents and child using exercises?
	What exercises/guidelines do you use?
	Do you view the joint creative work between the parent and the child as the therapy itself, or is it simply a starting point for a discussion?
	Do you offer the clients a chance to observe the artwork and learn from it?
	Is art present as well?
	Do the parents lead the sessions, or do you?
What happens during parent training?	Do you incorporate an art activity during parent training sessions as well?
	How do you ensure that the parents feel that their place as parents has not been jeopardized?
	How do parents respond to art during therapy with the child?
	What was the goal?
	What was the setting?
	How long did you meet?
	What happened in the therapy room?
Examples—please tell me about a therapeutic process that was successful and one that was ineffectual.	What was the cause of the failure/success?
	How do you decide whether therapy has been a success?
	Who decides on the termination of the therapeutic process?
What difficulties do you encounter when working in parent-child art psychotherapy?	Are you a mother/father?
	How does this help you?
How does the fact that you are a mother/father affect your role?	How does this challenge you?

Content Analysis of the Interviews

Phase I: Grounded Theory Coding

The 15 interviews were recorded and transcribed for content analysis using grounded theory (Glaser & Strauss, 1967). In the first stage of grounded theory analysis, called the open coding stage, we each worked separately, read the transcribed interviews, and highlighted the relevant themes that emerged from the data. The smallest unit of information was defined as a short sentence, and longer units could be as long as a whole paragraph. In the second stage of analysis, called the axial coding stage, we held a joint discussion, during which we defined the central categories and subcategories, and chose labels that corresponded and characterized each theme and content category. A narrative description of each category and the definition of the themes contained within them were also prepared, together with an excerpt from the interviews. The third stage, known as the selective coding stage, involved rereading all the interviews and reconsidering the extent to which the content expressed in the data is accurately reflected in the categories defined in stage 2. At the end of stage 3, the content in each category was fully defined in a way that incorporated all the information in the interviews.

Phase II: Category Content Confirmation

The final coding revealed that certain specific issues were only discussed in a few interviews, although they seemed to apply to all the therapists, such as the use of art-based interventions in the parent training sessions. For clarification, the 15 original therapists were re-contacted and 5 additional therapists were asked to participate, to better determine whether the information defined in each category was indeed relevant to the work of all the parent-child art therapists in the study (Lincoln & Guba, 1985). All were asked to assess the relevance of each category to their work on a scale ranging from 1 (content does not characterize my work) to 5 (content fully characterizes my work).

Chapters 3–7 present the information that emerged from the interviews, and describe the model of parent-child art psychotherapy as it is implemented in Israel.

Summary

- This chapter describes the data collection procedure used in this book in a study on the principles of parent-child art psychotherapy in Israel (sections have appeared in Regev & Snir, 2014, 2015).
- Twenty parent-child art therapists, all of whom specialize in this approach, were interviewed in two phases. The sample included nineteen women and one man, ranging in age from 36 to 61.

- The interviews with the therapists were semi-structured, which allowed the participants to express their perceptions of their work, and describe and illustrate their work through examples from their therapeutic practice.
- The 15 original interviews were used as a basis for content analysis implementing the principles of grounded theory to organize the data (Glaser & Strauss, 1967). In phase II, the 15 original parent-child art therapists as well as 5 additional participants were asked to rate the relevance of each category to their work as a control of the coding process.

Note

1 Some material presented in this book has already appeared in Regev and Snir (2014, 2015).

References

Glaser, B. G., & Strauss, A. L. (Eds). (1967). *The discovery of grounded theory: Strategies for qualitative research*. New York: Aldine.

Lincoln, Y. S., & Guba, E. G. (1985). *Naturalistic inquiry*. Newbury Park, CA: Sage.

McCracken, G. (1988). *The long interview*. Newbury Park, CA: Sage.

Regev, D., & Snir, S. (2014). Working with parent-child art psychotherapy. *The Arts in Psychotherapy*, *41*(5), 511–518.

Regev, D., & Snir, S. (2015). Objectives, interventions and challenges in parent-child art psychotherapy. *The Arts in Psychotherapy*, *42*, 50–56.

3 The Objectives of Parent-Child Art Psychotherapy

This chapter focuses on the therapeutic objectives of parent-child art psychotherapy. These objectives are established at the beginning of the therapeutic process but can develop and change accordingly throughout therapy. Individual objectives are established to serve a particular family's therapeutic needs. However, it is possible to focus more generally on objectives that art therapists often use in their work. These objectives stem from theoretical concepts behind this therapeutic approach. As part of our study, we asked art therapists to discuss the issues and goals related to therapy. This chapter explores how therapists view these objectives.

Setting Objectives

The field of art therapy has undergone considerable changes in the last few years and more therapists have started using the parent-child art psychotherapy model. In the past, parents who came with their children for therapy were not aware they could take part in the therapeutic process. Today, more parents inform the therapist even before the first therapy session whether they are interested in parent-child art psychotherapy. The objectives of parent-child art psychotherapy are normally related to the original reasons that led parents or teachers to refer a child to art therapy in the first place and tend to be connected to functional, learning, social, or other difficulties at home or at school. Nevertheless, it is unusual for parents or educators to specify at the onset that this relationship is central to the therapeutic process. Most therapists define the main objective of therapy as changing or improving the child's psychological well-being, behavior, and functioning. In order to achieve this change, there is a general consensus that the therapeutic process should focus on the relationship between the parent and the child, and the ways in which the parent perceives, understands, and behaves within the relationship with the child (Ben-Aaron, Harel, Kaplan, & Patt, 2001). However, the ultimate objective is not only to change the interactions within the relationship, but also the objective condition of the child in therapy.

In this chapter, we define four intermediate objectives that serve a central purpose in parent-child art psychotherapy (Regev & Snir, 2015). There is no one order to these intermediate objectives as regards their level of importance or value to therapy. The interventions used to achieve these objectives are described in greater detail in other chapters.

Objective 1: Creating Time and Space for Being Together

The first and perhaps most fundamental goal is related to the potential and value of parent-child art psychotherapy. When parent and child are simply together and present in a safe shared space that is both permanent and defined, this establishes a foundation for change in the relationship. This time slot becomes a unique occasion in their weekly schedules: a time when they know that they will be there for one another. In the therapy room, the therapist provides the parent and child with joint play activities, including art activities, which enable them to engage in collaborative interactions. Most therapists considered that the goal is to allow this form of interaction to reflect the relationship in its most natural state and should include activities that they usually do together. However, this form of quality time is seldom found in today's hectic lifestyles and therapists recommend filling this gap by enjoying activities together (Ginsburg, 2007). Today, many children have never experienced a positive joint environment with their parents such as drawing, playing, or even cooking. Being together allows parents to be with their children in an environment that fosters attentiveness and availability to the child (the parent is not busy at work or attending to siblings), while simultaneously engaging in an activity that encourages positive interactions (as opposed to other daily interactions where the parent instructs the child to do homework, or go take a shower).

One example of this is a father-daughter dyad who came for therapy. Most days, the father was not at home in the afternoon because he was so busy and he hardly knew his daughter. The therapist reported that during the first few sessions, it was very difficult to be with them in the therapy room because they argued and disagreed most of the time. The father did not want to be in the room and complained that he was uninterested and bored. A change took place when they began using scraps and ready-made materials to design a house together. In the following sessions, the therapist noticed how their mutual presence in the therapy room allowed for the establishment of a close relationship that also extended to joint activities outside it.

Objective 2: The Creation of a Playful Space in the Therapy Room

Similar to the Winnicottian approach with regard to the importance of the potential space (Moran, 1987; Winnicott, 1971), the second objective involves the creation of a space for play in the therapy room. This space allows for internal and interactive content to be expressed, and for new ways of coping to be established. Therapists are unanimous that inviting and encouraging the creation of a space for playfulness and creativity in therapy is crucially important. This space and the element of play can be extended to the everyday lives of the dyads beyond the therapy room. In the Winnicottian approach to therapy, playfulness is a way of life, and a means of creating a personal and interpersonal meeting place (Winnicott, 1971). Daily routine activities, such as eating, bathing, or getting ready for school, are presented in therapy as activities that can be fun and playful. One example of this can be seen in a dyad of a mother and her son with ADHD who struggled to express himself emotionally. He initially seemed unable to take part in play activities. His condition also affected his social skills. During their therapy sessions, the mother was trained how to develop and expand ludic moments with her son, who improved as therapy progressed.

Objective 3: Observing and Learning through Interactions Concerning the Self, the Other, and Their Interplay within a Relationship

Parent-child art therapists give parents and children the opportunity to observe their interactions and attend to their feelings and behavior. This enables parents to learn about themselves and their roles as parents, and to identify the internal representations that direct their perceptions of their child and their own actions. Parents are encouraged to observe their children. This allows them to distinguish between the child's needs and character, and their own perception of the child that stems from their relationship at younger ages. Buck, Dent-Brown, Parry, and Boote (2014), who examined the attitudes of parent-child art therapists in Britain, suggested that one of the key principles in therapy is to create a connection between the past and the present, historically, socially, and developmentally. Israeli therapists make an effort to find out about the parents' background, home, and extended family. Their work with the parents involves aiming for a better understanding of the perceptions, concerns, and complexities of the parent-child relationship that derives from these circumstances. As part of the parental training sessions, the therapist tries to guide the parents to engage in introspection to identify which reactions on the part of the child are related more to the parents' past or personal experiences in other significant relationships, and not to the child in his or her current state. The Buck et al. (2014) study also suggested that encouraging the child to observe and recognize feelings during interactions with parents should be one of the main objectives of therapy. The therapists here often mentioned that they encouraged children to observe themselves and the parent-child relationship, but that this reflective process should be adapted to the developmental abilities of the child.

This emphasis on reflective work in therapy is related to the growing interest in mentalization (Fonagy & Target, 1997), as discussed in Chapter 1. The notion of mentalization serves to develop the ability to understand and direct behavior and relationships through reflection on the self and the other with respect to one's mental world (e.g., one's feelings, perceptions, and thoughts). The parent-child art psychotherapy room gives parents and children a space to engage together in art-based interactions that mirror their relationship. This interaction forms the basis for observations by the therapist, the parent, and the child, as well as an exploration of perceptions of the self and others that occur in these relationships. After observations of the relationship and the ensuing insights, most therapists move to the assessment of additional responses, or alternative modes of communication. One therapist described parents who were in parent-child art psychotherapy to deal with their son's anxiety issues, which were also causing social problems. During therapy, it emerged that although the parents wanted their son to have a lot of friends, they themselves did not have a wide social circle outside of the family. Observing this helped them to understand the meaning of their child's behavior in a new and different way, and to accept their son and think of a variety of ways to support him both emotionally and socially.

Objective 4: Providing Information and Support to the Parents, the "Good Grandmother" Function

Therapists often use the expression the "good grandmother" to describe their role in relation to parents in parent-child art psychotherapy. This is also part of many parent-child psychotherapy models (e.g., see Harel, Kaplan, Avimeir-Patt, & Ben-Aaron, 2006; McDonough, 2000). The "good grandmother" defines the position of the therapist as regards the dyad in therapy, and relates specifically to the therapist's attitude toward the parents. Most therapists describe their primary role as providing support through empathy rather than judgment. In the literature, this function was originally dubbed "good grandmother transference" by Stern (1995, 1998) and related to the needs of the mother when she assumes the maternal role and becomes closer to other mothers, and in particular her own mother. Parent-child art therapists often encounter parents who lack a support system. Unlike in the past when women were supported by their mothers, most grandmothers are still at the peak of their careers when their children start their own families. They may also be dealing with old age issues and separation from their own parents and are often not sufficiently physically or emotionally available for their children. Thus, both young and new parents often feel that they lack the support and knowledge to raise their children and fulfill their role as parents.

By adopting this role, the therapist supports the parents' strengths and abilities, and conveys psycho-educational information about specific parenting functions and the child's development. The therapist also serves as a source of containment for the needs of the parent. This is usually directed at specific cases in which the parent encounters patterns of behavior by the child that appear incomprehensible to them, which in turn causes them to feel inadequate as parents of this child. Parents often tend to panic even with normative children who face normal developmental difficulties, such as temper tantrums at younger ages, fears, and concerns. They may find themselves responding to these issues with growing anxiety, which makes it difficult for the child to move through these life stages successfully and continue with normal development. For children with special needs, parents are often not aware of the scope and significance of the child's unique needs, which can further impair their understanding of what their child is experiencing. For example, a parent of a child with ADHD may understand the meaning of the disability in terms of the literature, but may not recognize the connection between the disability and specific social or organization problems at home. This can weaken the fabric of the relationship.

The therapist often utilizes his or her own personal experiences as a parent when adopting the role of the "good grandmother" in parent-child art psychotherapy. The therapist identifies parents who need another source of direction and support. As a part of this role, therapists attempt to present their own point of view in a way that will not impair, threaten, or compete with the position of the parent (Harel et al., 2006). This function of the "good grandmother" help parents distinguish between different interpretations of their children's behavior and expectations that are not age-appropriate. In one instance, a therapist received an emergency call from parents whose daughter was suddenly not willing to go to school. During the first stage of the therapeutic process, the therapist made herself readily available to these parents who needed support almost daily due to the complexity of the situation. In this example, the therapist became an accompanying figure, and adopted the role of grandmother for this family at a challenging time in their lives.

Summary

- The main objective of parent-child art psychotherapy is to create a form of change or improvement in the child's psychological well-being, behavior, and functioning.
- There are four intermediate objectives that serve this central objective: (1) creating a time and space for being together; (2) the creation of a playful space in the therapy room where internal and interactive content can be expressed, and new ways of coping may be formed; (3) observing and learning from interaction concerning the self, others, and the relationship between them; and (4) providing information and support to the parent, the "good grandmother" function.

References

Ben-Aaron, M., Harel, J., Kaplan, H., & Patt, R. (2001). *Mother-child and father-child psychotherapy: A manual for the treatment of relational disturbances in childhood*. London and Philadelphia, PA: Whurr.

Buck, E. T., Dent-Brown, K., Parry, G., & Boote, J. (2014). Dyadic art psychotherapy: Key principles, practices and competences. *The Arts in Psychotherapy*, *41*, 163–173.

Fonagy, P., & Target, M. (1997). Attachment and reflective function: Their role in self organization. *Development and Psychopathology*, *9*, 679–900.

Ginsburg, K. R. (2007). The importance of play in promoting healthy child development and maintaining strong parent-child bonds. *Pediatrics*, *119*(1), 182–191.

Harel, J., Kaplan, H., Avimeir-Patt, R., & Ben-Aaron, M. (2006). The child's active role in mother-child, father-child psychotherapy: A psychodynamic approach to the treatment of relational disturbances. *Psychology and Psychotherapy: Theory, Research and Practice*, 79(1), 23–36.

McDonough, S. C. (2000). Interaction guidance: An approach for difficult to engage families. In C. Zeanah (Ed.), *Handbook of infant mental health* (pp. 485–493). New York, NY: Guildford Press.

Moran, G. S. (1987). Some functions of play and playfulness: A developmental perspective. *The Psychoanalytic Study of the Child*, *42*, 11–29.

Regev, D., & Snir, S. (2015). Objectives, interventions and challenges in parent-child art psychotherapy. *The Arts in Psychotherapy*, *42*, 50–56.

Stern, D. N. (1995). *The motherhood constellation*. New York, NY: Basic Books.

Stern, D. N. (1998). Mothers' emotional needs. *Pediatrics*, *102* (Supplement E1), 1250–1252.

Winnicott, D. W. (1971). *Playing and reality*. London: Tavistock.

4 The Parent-Child Art Psychotherapy Setting

The previous chapter addressed the definition of the objectives of parent-child art psychotherapy. The goal of this chapter is to suggest a suitable structure for this therapy setting. In this context, the term "setting" refers to the following: the presence of the parents in the therapy room, adjusting the therapy room to the needs and objectives of therapy, adapting the type of art materials best suited for creative work, the storage and care of the artworks, and finally the issue of displaying the artworks from other clients or keeping them confidential.

Alternating Therapeutic Work with Parents

The Haifa parent-child psychotherapy model underscores the importance of the presence of both parents with the child in therapy (Ben-Aaron, Harel, Kaplan, & Patt, 2001). According to this model, the presence of the father in therapy is of great significance. His role in the normal development of the child and the success of therapy has been discussed in the context of the development of the three-way relationship (Benjamin, 2004). The father is perceived as a key figure in the development of individual autonomy (Mahler, Pine, & Bergman, 1975) and plays an important role in enabling the child to detach from symbiosis with the mother, as well as in promoting general inquiry and encounters with the outside world (Abelin, 1975). The father is also viewed as the figure who helps to set boundaries (Barrows, 2004) and develop gender identity if the child is a male (Blos, 1984). It is worth noting that in actual practice as mirrored by the professional literature on parent-child psychotherapy (Kaplan, Harel, & Avimeir-Patt, 2010) as a whole, including the father in therapy is difficult. Even though most therapists insist on the presence of the father in therapy, it is evident that in some therapeutic settings, particularly those that take place in public settings, only the mother takes part. In our experience, there are two main reasons for this. The first involves the fact that fathers in some families in Israel work longer hours than mothers, and are therefore less available for meetings of this kind, specifically in public settings where the therapeutic work is habitually carried out in the morning hours. Second, from our work experience in training art therapists in the Israeli context, we have found that since most of the therapists are women, it is often easier for the therapist to ask mothers to be part of parent-child psychotherapy and parent training. This may be the case because they feel more comfortable having a woman-to-woman discussion, or because they feel that fathers are more intimidating, more opposed to the therapeutic process, or articulate themselves in an unfamiliar manner to female therapists.

Despite these hurdles, therapists need to grasp the importance of maintaining the recommended structure of the Haifa parent-child psychotherapy model. In this structure, the parents alternate therapy sessions, such that the child attends one session with the mother and the next session with the father. In addition, the therapist meets with both parents once every three sessions for parent training without the presence of the child. When the child comes from a single-parent family, or from a family of divorced parents, changes are made in the structure of the therapy sessions to better fit the unique needs of each family.

Finally, concerning therapy in public settings where there are issues of time and budget, parent training can replace a regular therapy session. However, and whenever possible, it is preferable to convene these training sessions at a different time to avoid interrupting the child's sequence of therapy sessions.

The Therapy Room

The therapy room is the space in which the therapy takes place. It can be viewed as the container that holds the therapist, and helps the therapist to preserve the therapeutic environment. The therapy room helps the therapist exploit the range of possibilities available in art psychotherapy by defining specific work areas devolved to different therapeutic functions. The walls of the room define the space in which one can remain during therapy, and thus serve as a boundary that defines the location of therapy and act as a barrier that ensures privacy from the outside world. The features of the therapy room and the atmosphere it projects affect the people within the space, either consciously or unconsciously, thus making the design of the room very important. In public clinics, the therapist has less latitude to modulate the structure and properties of the therapy room, and many therapists report experiencing difficulties in such settings. In a private clinic, the design of the room is affected by the personality and perceptions of the therapist, and reflects the ways in which the therapist makes his or her presence felt in the room. For example, some therapists may choose to hang their academic diplomas on the wall, which underscores their rank as professionals in their field. The choice of pictures and furniture, whether materials are put away neatly or some untidiness is allowed, as well as cultural characteristics, together convey the therapist's personality and the way the therapist would like to be seen by the client.

The metaphorical aspects of the therapy room are reflected in the way the room and its furnishings serve as representations of a holding environment and the therapist's body, which are associated with the mother figure (Winnicott, 1965). In this environment, clients can project feelings and emotions in a way that allows them to be processed (Dorani, 2016). Most art therapists who work according to the parent-child psychotherapy model describe the therapy room setting as having a play area, a rug, and a worktable that is big enough for both the parent and the child to sit on chairs appropriate for their age. The table should allow enough range of motion for the parent and child to be able to switch places and move around. In some clinics, there are drawing boards that can be used standing up, which enables a greater range of motion, as well as the ability to change positions and distances from the page (Hazut, 2014). This setup lets parent and child switch positions on the page, work close to one another, or stand back and look at the work from afar. Drawing while standing has aspects of physical tension, and on a symbolic level enables a sense of control over the work as opposed to a sense of weakness, helplessness, and victimization (Hazut, 2000). Additionally, in some clinics, therapists stress the importance of creating a seating area with poufs or cushions that serves as the space where the session begins and ends with a joint discussion between parent, child, and therapist. The use of a large room for parent-child art psychotherapy appears to allow for versatility and the division of space into different work areas. This makes it possible to work together at the table, draw together on a board, play together on the carpet, and have a joint conversation at the beginning and end of every session in the same space.

The art room provides an empowering, holding, and safe space, which serves according to the art therapy theoretical literature, as a container in which mental transformations can take place through the use of art materials (Killick, 2010). Most art therapists who work according to the parent-child psychotherapy model mention there is a large supply of art materials and games stored in the therapy room within children's easy reach. Some materials and games are kept in closed closets to avoid overstimulation, whereas others are visible and accessible in the room. Having a sink in the room is considered to help the therapist observe the parent and child during routine activities such as hand-washing. Most therapists emphasize the importance of a permanent setting in terms of room arrangement, available art materials, and seating arrangements, which emphasize the proximity of the child and parent, and give them a place at the table across from the therapist. However, many art therapists stated that they often adapt the therapy room before a session with a parent-child dyad to meet its specific needs. For example, the therapist can display the dyad's artwork in the room, or put out specific art materials that specific clients expressed interest in using, conceal other materials that the therapist believes are not appropriate for the dyad, place the chairs closer together, and so on. Alternatively, the therapist may hide art materials or utensils that are inappropriate for a specific parent-child dyad, or arrange the chairs to be closer to each other, and so on.

Art Materials

Most art therapists using the parent-child psychotherapy model emphasized the advantages of having a variety of art materials available in the art therapy room, and stated that any material can be adapted to their work. These materials include various kinds of paint (oil, gouache, and finger paints), clay, Silly Putty, paper, cardboard and newspapers, pictures, paper mâché, objects that can be used to create ready-made art, wool, fabric, natural materials, wire, mesh, plaster, polystyrene balls, pipe cleaners, glitter, sequins, wooden skewers, and others. All of these materials belong to the wide range of possible art work with structured and controlled materials, such as pencils and markers, or liquid substances that are harder to control and can get the user dirty, but also promote play, such as gouache or finger paints (also referred to as regressive materials).

The art materials used in the therapy room are an additional player in the relationship between the therapist and the client, and should be considered within the therapeutic contract. The therapeutic contract specifies what is permitted or prohibited in the therapy room. Different therapists relate differently to this component as a function of the client (e.g., whether it is appropriate to expose the client to a variety of materials or a narrow selection, whether the client should use controlled or more regressive materials, or whether a cutting tool should be present in the room), the therapist's approach (how appropriate is it to allow the client a variety of experiences with a range of art materials), and the container in which the therapy takes place—the art therapy room (what the client is allowed to do in the therapy room in terms of untidiness and getting things dirty).

Some therapists suggested that the clients should be gradually and carefully exposed to the variety of materials in the room. This position stems from the belief that an abundance of materials may confuse clients and hinder their ability to express themselves (Moon, 2010). Occasionally, parent and child find art materials that are unique to their parent-child dyad. Examples may include skill and expertise in working with wood with a hammer and nails, or perhaps cooking and baking, which is only possible if the therapy room allows for this form of creativity. Recently, we have been thinking of expanding the use of recycled materials, both for economic and ecological reasons, such as working with cardboard cut from boxes, or old newspapers, which can replace commercial, store-bought white paper. The use of boxes as raw material has great potential in therapy, as they can be containers, treasure chests, secret spaces, and so on (Farrell-Kirk, 2001).

Used paper can be turned into paper mâché, and ceramic or glass fragments can be used for mosaics and more. These ideas are especially important in public clinics where budget constraints may lead to a smaller selection of art materials.

The Exposure of the Client's Works

One of the issues that art therapists frequently address in both private clinics and public settings is the exposure of artworks created by other clients. In the context of parent-child psychotherapy, this can become even more crucial since the parents are also involved in making the artworks in the therapy room. Therapists have developed two different approaches to deal with this problem. The first is to keep all artwork confidential to prevent overstimulation and interference with the parent-child therapeutic process. Typically, before each session, the therapist takes out the previous piece of artwork the parent and child created in the therapy room together. Alternatively, the therapist displays the artworks of all the clients, thus enabling the clients to see the works of others and pick up on ideas for their own artwork. This creates a nonverbal dialogue with the other clients and prompts the client to realize that the room is used by other families as well. One example of this involved the dialogue that took place between a first-grader and a sixth-grader, in two separate parent-child dyads, who never met each other. In one session, the younger child was exposed to artwork created by the older child. The younger child perceived this artwork to be a mansion and drew a security guard for the property. The older child, who had drawn a football field, added an additional security guard to keep the first one company. This dialogue only took place between the artworks, and because of this exchange, both clients and their parents waited excitedly each week to see the changes that had been made in the other client's artwork. A similar approach was recently introduced by Bat-Or (2015), who argues that the dialogue between the artworks of children with ADHD can be a form of significant therapeutic intervention. Thus, the decisions relating to issues of confidentiality or display (Hazut & Siano, 2007) should be made by the therapist, who needs to take the communicative qualities of the artworks, the client's needs, and their own preferences into consideration.

Storing and Keeping Client's Artworks

An additional topic related to the therapy setting and art therapy in general, but which has slightly different meaning in parent-child art psychotherapy, is the issue of keeping clients' artworks. Since the parent and child create something together in the therapy room, some may ask to take the artworks home at the end of a session. However, most therapists stated that it was important to keep the works in the therapy room, which is also standard practice in the profession (Hazut & Siano, 2007). This way, the therapist makes it clear that the artworks, including their positive and negative features, all have a place in the therapy room. We believe that during the therapeutic process, it is ideal to keep the artworks in the therapy room where they are protected from damage or harmful criticism. However, it is important that therapists consider the needs of the parent and child in therapy and recognize that it is occasionally acceptable to allow them to take artworks home that were made during therapy sessions. There may be situations where the artwork that was created in the therapy room symbolizes an achievement in the parent-child relationship. For example, the parent and child may experience a unique moment of shared enjoyment. The parent and child may want to transfer this experience to the home, the shared family space, and extend its effect from art to reality. Under these circumstances, the artwork may be a symbolic transitional object, and the therapist should consider allowing the artwork to be taken home. In other situations, an esthetic artwork may reflect the parent and child's capabilities and qualities and lead to further forms of appreciation. The desire to take a piece of artwork is thus connected to a desire to display it to others and be encouraged by others' reactions. For example, a father and son who worked on a spaceship project during therapy wanted to share the artwork with the mother and show their enjoyment in the creative process. In such cases, the therapist needs to consider whether the external environment is supportive, and if so, can let the artwork leave the room. Another case is when the artwork has an important message that applies to a wider audience, and the creators want to show it to the parties in question. For example, during a number of different therapy sessions, a mother and her daughter created a series of clay figures that represented their family members. These included the mother, the father, the daughter, and the two brothers. This series possibly reflected the mother and daughter's need for a supportive family environment and the therapist consented when they asked to take the work home. Finally, there may be cases where the parent and child make a gift for someone who is not present in the therapy room. For example, if a client makes a card for a grandmother for the holidays, the therapist can encourage and validate the parent and child's ability to create something together, and allow them to give it to the intended recipient.

Summary

- In the parent-child psychotherapy model, the therapeutic process takes place in the presence of both parents, and the child alternates therapy sessions with the mother or with the father. In addition, every third session, the therapist meets with both parents for training purposes without the presence of the child.
- *The therapy room*: Most art therapists who work according to the parent-child psychotherapy model describe the therapy room as typically

comprising a play area, a rug, and a table that is large enough to seat both the parent and the child on appropriately sized chairs. In some of the therapy rooms, there is an upright drawing board. The art materials and games are stored in the therapy room at a height that is accessible to the child. In addition, some therapists emphasize the importance of creating a seating area where the session begins and ends with a joint discussion between parent, child, and therapist.

- *The art materials*: Most art therapists who work according to the parent-child psychotherapy model mentioned the large variety of art materials available in the art therapy room, and also stated that any material can be adapted for the purposes of creative work.
- *The exposure of clients' works*: According to one approach, before the therapy session, the therapist only displays the artworks of the parent and child dyad attending the specific therapy session to prevent over-stimulation and interference in the therapeutic process. Alternatively, the therapist displays the artworks of other clients in the therapy room, thus allowing for the creation of nonverbal dialogues with other clients.
- *Storing and keeping clients' artworks*: Most therapists believe that it is important to keep the artworks created by the parent and the child in the therapy room, since this shows that the artworks, including their positive and negative features, all have a place. However, under certain circumstances, the therapist may allow the parent and child to take their artworks home.

References

Abelin, E. L. (1975). Some further observations and comments on the earliest role of the father. *International Journal of Psycho-Analysis, 56*, 293–302.

Barrows, P. (2004). Fathers and families: Locating the ghost in the nursery. *Infant Mental Health Journal, 25*(5), 408–423.

Bat-Or, M. (2015). Art therapy with AD/HD children: Exploring possible selves via art. In E. E. Kourkoutas, A. Hart, & A. Mouzaki (Eds.), *Innovative practice and interventions for children and adolescents with psychosocial difficulties, disorders, and disabilities* (pp. 373–389). Newcastle upon Tyne: Cambridge Scholar.

Ben-Aaron, M., Harel, J., Kaplan, H., & Patt, R. (2001). *Mother-child and father-child psychotherapy: A manual for the treatment of relational disturbances in childhood.* London and Philadelphia, PA: Whurr.

Benjamin, J. (2004). *Beyond doer and done to: An intersubjective view of thirdness.* Lecture given at Tel-Aviv University.

Blos, P. (1984). Son and father. *Journal of the American Psychoanalytic Association, 32*, 301–324.

Dorani, H. (2016). *Art therapy rooms in schools in the education system.* (Unpublished Master's Dissertation). University of Haifa, Israel. (In Hebrew).

Farrell-Kirk, R. (2001). Secrets, symbols, synthesis, and safety: The role of boxes in art therapy. *American Journal of Art Therapy*, 39(3), 88–92.

Hazut, T. (2000). Black also has shades: Art as a ritual in dealing with loss and bereavement. *The Arts Therapies*, 3(1), 107–129. (In Hebrew).

Hazut, T. (2014). "Haifa approach" to visual arts therapy. In R. Berger (Ed.), *Arts: The heart of therapy* (pp. 192–232). Kiryat Bialik: Ach Publishing.

Hazut, T., & Siano, J. (2007). Ethical issues in the creative arts therapies; Haifa University, the Graduate School of Creative Arts Therapies. In G. Shefler, Y. Achman, & G. Wiell (Eds.), *Ethics in counseling and therapeutic professions* (pp. 424–441). Jerusalem: Magnes Press. (In Hebrew).

Kaplan, H., Harel, Y., & Avimeir-Patt, R. (2010). *Dyadic therapy: An encounter between the therapeutic act and theory.* Department of Psychology, University of Haifa. (In Hebrew).

Killick, K. (2010). The art room as container in analytical art psychotherapy with patients in psychotic states. In A. Gilroy & G. McNeilly (Eds.), *The changing shape of art therapy: New developments in theory and practice* (pp. 99–114). London: Jessica Kingsley.

Mahler, M. S., Pine, F., & Bergman, A. (1975). *The psychological birth of the human infant.* New York, NY: Basic Books.

Moon, C. (2010). *Materials and media in art therapy: Critical understandings of diverse artistic vocabularies.* New York, NY: Routledge.

Winnicott, D. W. (1965). *Ego distortion in terms of true and false self. The maturational process and the facilitating environment: Studies in the theory of emotional development* (pp. 140–157). New York, NY: International Universities Press.

5 The Role of the Parent-Child Art Therapist

This chapter discusses the role of the parent-child art therapist. It explores the key interventions in therapy and how these relate to the primary objectives of the parent-child art psychotherapy process (see Chapter 3). The intervention techniques used by parent-child art therapists need to take place in a space that allows for flexibility in terms of planning the therapeutic process and also shows sensitivity to the child's family history, the child's and therapist's cultural backgrounds, and the personal experiences of those participating in therapy (Buck, Dent-Brown, Parry, & Boote, 2014). Thus, the goal in this chapter is not to formulate a single work protocol, but rather to present ideas and interventions that art therapists can adapt to specific parent-child dyads in therapy, based on their professional judgment. This chapter outlines the general principles. More specific intervention techniques and guidelines for creating a joint painting are presented in Chapters 9–13.

The Gradual Expansion of Play Facilitated by Work with Art Materials

Many art therapists we interviewed who work according to the parent-child psychotherapy model indicated that at the start of the therapeutic process, they usually ask the parent and the child to interact in the therapy room together, as they do usually. To lessen the anxiety that can be associated with the start of therapy, they may suggest that the clients work with art materials that are relatively dry and easy to control such as markers, pencils, or crayons, all of which provide a sense of greater control and reduce anxiety (Moon, 2010; Snir & Regev, 2013).

However, at a later stage of therapy and while considering the objective of introducing play into the therapy room, some of the therapists mentioned that the art materials they offer to clients are presented in a way that gradually increases the amount of play that is permitted and encouraged in their presence. As mentioned above, art therapists tend initially to suggest materials such as pencils and markers, which provide a sense of control and confidence. Art materials that give the creator more freedom are gradually introduced into therapy and can act as play agents (Luria, 2002; Snir & Regev, 2013). Gouache paint, clay, or finger paints are materials that are difficult to control. They often leak, mix with other colors, and get the users dirty. When working with these materials, the creator may find unintentional marks or shapes on the page or the table. Hence, these less easily controlled materials can function as partners "who have something to say." At the beginning of the therapeutic process, the parent may perceive these playful materials as threatening, but over time, as both the relationship and a sense of security develop in therapy, these materials can be used successfully.

Shaping the Therapeutic Space Using Structured Exercises

One of the objectives of the therapeutic model is to create a time and space for the parent and child to be together. One of the most frequently recurring questions is how to build and encourage this sense of togetherness. Particularly at the beginning of the therapeutic process, but also when the process stagnates, it is advisable to start with structured activities that ease entry into the shared space, reduce levels of anxiety, and serve as a basis for change within the relationship. The parent and child begin the parent-child art psychotherapy process together; however, in many cases the parent has not engaged with art materials for many years and may feel anxious at the start of the shared activity. The therapists we interviewed stated that structured activities help reduce this tension and make the start of the therapeutic process much easier for parent and child.

In the next few chapters, we describe a variety of exercises that can help parent and child feel more confident at the beginning of therapy or in other situations in which the therapist feels the need for intervention. Creating a shared therapeutic space can involve exercises that encourage both joint creative art-making and individual work. For example, joint work is appropriate for a parent-child dyad who rarely spend time together because of the parent's work schedule, or when interactions elicit emotional issues with one or more members of the dyad (e.g., when a child reminds parents of parts of themselves they do not like). By contrast, individual work is appropriate for a symbiotic parent-child dyad whose fusion does not leave adequate room for separation, and where the parent and child need to learn how to act and flourish in a separate space.

Some therapists reported that they themselves take part in the initial art-making at the beginning of therapy to reduce the levels of anxiety. The therapist's decision depends on the ability of both the parent and the child to act within this triad, as well as issues that this additional presence may raise in therapy. The presence of a "third object" is described in the literature as crucial to the development of separation within the relationship (Mahler, Pine, & Bergman, 1975) and in terms of the child's ability to perceive an additional facet of his or her relationship with the parent, as seen from the perspective of the other (Kaplan, Harel, & Avimeir-Patt, 2010). This leads to different levels of togetherness (Benjamin, 2004), the development of ambivalence, and diversified perspectives on reality (Britton, 1992). This type of interaction may be useful in the case of single parents. In these cases, the therapist serves as a significant "third object," thus enabling both parent and child to experience and construct a different perspective of their relationship.

Since one of the objectives of parent-child psychotherapy is the creation of a playful space within the therapy room, another situation in which the therapist can structure the guidelines for joint work or suggest art exercises is when the therapeutic process stagnates and a playful space is not established.

Creating a Joint Painting

In joint painting activities, the parent and child share the same space on a single page and draw together. In most parent-child art psychotherapy sessions, the creation of a joint painting is the central therapeutic technique, and this topic will be addressed in the following chapters. The assumption underlying the use of this technique is that the space of the page reflects a shared living space. Due to the limited size of the page and its scarce resources, and similar to real-life circumstances, the parent and child are forced to share this space in a way that often reveals how they function within their relationship (Snir & Wiseman, 2010). There are two primary ways in which the joint painting reveals features about the parent-child relationship. The interaction between the parent and child while making the joint painting may reflect the type of interaction that commonly takes place between them, and this allows for the observation of the parent-child relationship (Markman-Zinemanas, 2011). This new and unfamiliar drawing space can maintain but also promote change in the relationship and kindle an element of enjoyment, which can be directed to other spheres of life. Second, self-representations, representations of the other, and representations of the relationship are reflected in the art-making as well as the artwork, and shed light on the internal working models of parent and child (Snir & Hazut, 2012).

The instructions for joint work activities can vary as a function of the issues, the point in time of therapy, or specific instances. Many of the instructions are listed in the final chapters of this book. At other times, the therapist gives no instructions for the joint painting, and the parent and child are simply given a page and art materials to use. The page size can vary from A4 to a larger sheet. The factors that influence the choice of the size of the page have to do with the need to provide a larger space (A1 sheet) or reduce it and create intimacy (A4 sheet). The choice of suitable art materials depends as well on the objectives of the activity, the artistic abilities of the parent and child, and the size of the page. Liquid gouache paints are more suitable for larger sheets, and less suitable for maintaining boundaries and separation between the creators. On the other hand, pencils and markers, which are materials that are easier to control, allow for the creation of clear, pure images, as well as better control of the marks and contour lines and the preservation of personal boundaries. Oil pastels allow the creator to switch between contour lines and marks to create a defined shape, but also encourage the use of touch, dabbing, smearing, and blending. This is why therapists often make pastels available for joint painting. The implications and significance of creating a joint painting are addressed in Chapters 8–12, and include a description of the intervention techniques.

Expressions of Aggression in the Therapy Room

A key issue in relationship-building is whether the therapist should prohibit certain types of violent behavior in the therapy room. To enable the expression of typical characteristic behavior, therapists may allow clients to destroy an artwork or to yell, since these manifestations probably emerge in other circumstances between parent and child, and can enable observation, discussion, understanding, and more suitable behavior. The art therapists interviewed here said they accepted interactions that included expressions of aggression in the therapy room to better understand what transpires in these situations, which they viewed as a mirror of other areas of life. However, most parent-child art therapists also set limits on certain behaviors in the therapy room and even predefine these restrictions, including physical violence that could harm those present or damage the therapy room. However, the parent-child art psychotherapy room provides a number of alternatives for the expression of anger and aggression. Kramer (1958) made it clear that artwork has great value on a subliminal level when socially improper urges are expressed through creativity. She believed that art-making utilizes forms of energy that are generated by human impulses, which are then channeled into a creative and constructive form.

The idea of encouraging the expression of the relationship in all its forms, while avoiding actual destruction in the therapy room, is based on an art therapy theory that draws on Kris' concept of regression in the service of the ego (Kris, 1952). Although Kramer did not let her clients destroy their artworks as an act of symbolic destruction, in Kris' approach, the idea of loss of control and the destruction of something may have a therapeutic value when destruction takes place on a symbolic level, such as with art materials (Shapira, 2005). For example, one of the therapists in the study described a situation where a parent and child created a clay monster together during one therapy session. The work was divided into sections and they made different parts. Toward the end of the session, the child was not satisfied with the outcome and wanted to smash it. He seemed to be frightened by the monster, who reflected threatening and frightening features of his inner world that he wanted to get rid of by destroying the monster. The therapist prompted the parent and child to talk about it. When the parent agreed, the therapist authorized the parent and child to destroy the artwork together, which they did with cries of joy. The regressive value of the symbolic destruction of the monster, together with the support of the parent, appeared to have positively impacted the child as well as the parent-child dyad.

Joint Observation

As described in Chapter 3, one of the objectives of parent-child psychotherapy is to encourage the parent and the child to observe and pay attention to their interactions to learn more about themselves, one another, and their relationship. During parent-child art psychotherapy, this observation phase often occurs when the participants talk about their joint painting. The therapist directs the observation process and provides the parent and child with a phenomenological rephrasing of what they see in the artwork (Snir & Wiseman, 2010). However, most therapists noted that they preferred to have the art-makers make interpretations rather than providing a description themselves. One of the therapists described a girl who gradually took control of her mother's section of the page and hardly left her any room to draw, although the mother acquiesced. When the therapist talked about what took place during the joint work and asked the mother what she saw, the mother realized that she had allowed her daughter to take control of almost all the shared space, and she understood the importance of protecting herself and her personal boundaries. Reflection through art that leaves room for interpretation or insights on the part of the client is based on the phenomenological approach to art therapy (Betensky, 1995), the psychoanalytical approach to art therapy (Naumburg, 1966), and is also supported by the Winnicottian approach to interpretation in psychoanalytic therapy (Aron, 1992).

Most therapists emphasized that in addition to the observation of the artwork, they prompt the participants to recall the joint creative process in their minds by asking them to specify who painted which elements and when during the sequence. During this process, the therapists ask the parent and child to state what they see, who they think drew over more space on the page, who showed initiative, who made the decisions, who led the creative process, and who was being led. The parent and child are asked to describe their emotions and feelings during the joint activity. This enables the parent and child to examine the relative contribution of each on the page, the power relations, and typical behavior (Snir & Wiseman, 2010). According to most therapists, these interventions help direct the parent to observe the child, and acknowledge the child's capabilities, unique characteristics, and needs, which in turn strengthens the parent's reflective ability.

The Art Therapist's Reflective Contribution

Most of the therapists reported that they often adopted a position of reflection and mediation. As part of this role, they described situations in which they expressed the ideas and issues of those who were not heard in the relationship: they attempted to express the child's voice and needs that were not understood by the parent, and vice versa. One of the therapists described a therapy session in which the father and child were present. During the session, the child played in the sandbox, grabbed toy soldiers, and said to his father: "Choose if you want to be the good guys or the bad guys." The father answered: "No, you pick first, and I'll take what's left." The boy insisted that the father choose first, and the therapist reflected to the father how important it was for the child to have a father who makes decisions. The child wanted a father who had command and control.

Examining Alternative Responses

The next step involves the examination of additional responses or alternative modes of communication. The objective, which is based on observation of the relationship, is to give the parent and child an opportunity to observe which patterns of responses lead to unwanted results, and an opportunity to consider alternative response patterns. It is possible to suggest a type of change within the relationship and teach the parent-child dyad how to apply this joint thinking process to other facets of their lives. One of the therapists addressed a difficult situation that she encountered with a mother and child. The mother and her 7-year-old daughter described an incident that happened to them the previous week. The mother expected to get help from her daughter, but the daughter did not comply. The discussion about the event revived the fight in the therapy room, and the mother said very harsh words to her daughter. In the drawing the girl made, she tried to express how she felt in the situation and explained that she was involved in a game when she was suddenly expected to help her mother, and therefore she did not respond accordingly. The therapist tried to find out how the mother felt when she was refused help by her daughter, as well as to try to think of alternative ways of asking for help, and expressing her dissatisfaction with her daughter's reaction. The therapist described how this method was effective in helping them to progress from action to observation of their behavior and a discussion about their dilemma. At a later stage, they were able to restrain their reactions and act differently.

Positive Moments of Meeting

Most therapists stressed the importance they gave to positive behavior and moments of meeting when this took place during therapy sessions, and used this as a way to strengthen these aspects of the relationship. This idea was also defined by Buck et al. (2014) as a key function of parent-child art psychotherapy. One of the therapists described an example when working with a child and his father. The child and his father both drew on an A1 sheet of paper that was hanging on the wall. After multiple parent training sessions and the father's difficulty to connect with his son, the father showed empathy and tried to connect with the child through the drawing. The boy said to his father: "Paint like that, do this," and the father responded to the needs of the child. Then the father asked his son: "Am I doing this well?" and the boy answered: "Yes, daddy it's fine, I'm pleased." It was a moment of meeting, and the art therapist intervened and said: "It looks like you trust your daddy." The boy responded: "Yes, he's my dad, he's good at everything he does." This was a very significant moment of meeting for both of them; they realized for the first time how they both see one another, believe in one another, and appreciate one another. This intervention is based on the phenomenological approach to art therapy, which emphasizes the abilities and strengths of the client (Hazut & Hesse, personal communication), and is consistent with analytical approaches that emphasize the importance of shared moments of pleasure during moments of growth (Alvarez, 1992).

Modeling

With regard to the objective of providing information and support to parents, most therapists stated how important it was for them to express their points of view in a way that did not detract from the position of the parent, or threaten or compete with it (Harel, Kaplan, Avimeir-Patt, & Ben-Aaron, 2006). One of the methods that almost every therapist mentioned to achieve this objective was the technique of modeling, where the therapist acts in a particular way in the therapy room in front of the child. This technique allows the therapist to present an alternative means of communication. One of the therapists gave the example of a boy in parent-child art psychotherapy. He asked her: "Can I show you something that I did to my father?" and then he bent her finger backwards. The day before, the boy did the same thing to his father and his father screamed from pain and then reprimanded him. The therapist did not let the boy bend her finger entirely, but pulled her hand away and responded: "What are you doing? It really, really hurts! What were you trying to do?" The boy turned around and hid in the corner of the room and said: "I don't want anyone to see me, I'm ashamed, I don't want them to see my artworks." The therapist sat next to the boy and said: "You're terribly ashamed that you suddenly had a very, very naughty thought that you would hurt me, and that you would test your strength against mine and I reacted the way I did, and you're ashamed that you wanted to hurt me." The mother responded to the situation by saying: "If this had happened in front of me, I would have screamed at him and become worried that he was acting aggressively, and be afraid that this probably happens in other situations as well. I would have become very anxious and then nothing would have happened." Through the technique of modeling, the therapist demonstrated how to react differently. She reasoned with the boy and verbalized some of the reasons for his acting out.

Summary

- The gradual expansion of play that is facilitated by work with art materials is important when the therapist and the parent-child dyad are starting to get to know each other. Many forms of anxiety can be relieved by encouraging clients to work with controlled and relatively dry materials such as markers, pencils, or crayons. However, as the therapeutic process progresses, the clients are gradually presented with art materials that allow for the expansion of play in therapy.
- *Shaping the therapeutic space using structured exercises*: In particular at the beginning of the therapeutic process, but also when the process stagnates, it is advisable to start with structured activities to ease the transition into the shared space to reduce levels of anxiety, which can serve as a basis for change within the relationship. Some therapists take part in art work at the beginning of the therapeutic process to reduce the level of anxiety.
- *Creating a joint painting*: In most parent-child art psychotherapy sessions, the creation of a joint painting is a central therapeutic technique. The basic idea is that the space of the page reflects the shared living space. Methods of instruction for joint work can vary, and there are many forms of artwork entering into this process.
- *Expressions of aggression in the therapy room*: Many art therapists find value in interactions that include expressions of aggression in the therapy room because they shed light on what transpires outside of the therapy room. However, most parent-child art therapists do not allow certain behaviors, and may even predefine these boundaries. At the same time, the parent-child art psychotherapy room provides many alternatives for expressions of anger and aggression.
- *Joint observation*: Joint observation of the art work often involves having parent and child observe and discuss their joint painting. Most therapists stated that they preferred the creators to make the interpretations themselves. Therapists also try to encourage the parent-child dyad to recall the joint creative process, and ask them to specify who painted which elements and when.
- *The art therapist's reflective contribution*: Therapists described situations in which they expressed the ideas and issues that are not heard in the relationship, and they attempt to express the child's voice and needs that have not been understood by the parent, and vice versa.

- *Examining alternative responses*: Parent and child are encouraged to talk about patterns of behavior that emerge in the session that lead to unwanted results and then think about productive alternative responses.
- *Positive moments of meeting*: Most therapists ascribed crucial importance to positive behavior and moments of meeting during therapy sessions and used this as a way to strengthen these aspects of the relationship.
- *Modeling*: Most therapists stated how important it was for therapists to express their points of view in a way that does not detract from the position of the parent, or threaten or compete with it. One of the methods that almost every therapist mentioned to achieve this objective was the technique of modeling, where the therapist acts and reacts in a particular way in the therapy room in front of the child in the presence of the parent.

References

Alvarez, A. (1992). *Live company*. London: Routledge.

Aron, L. (1992). Interpretation as expression of the analyst's subjectivity. *Psychoanalytic Dialogues*, 2(4), 475–507.

Benjamin, J. (2004). *Beyond doer and done to: An intersubjective view of thirdness*. Lecture given at Tel-Aviv University.

Betensky, M. (1995). *What do you see? Phenomenology of therapeutic art expression*. London: Jessica Kingsley.

Britton, R. (1992). The Oedipus situation and the depressive position. In R. Anderson (Ed.), *Clinical lectures on Klein and Bion* (pp. 34–45). London and New York, NY: Tavistock/Routledge.

Buck, E. T., Dent-Brown, K., Parry, G., & Boote, J. (2014). Dyadic art psychotherapy: Key principles, practices and competences. *The Arts in Psychotherapy*, 41, 163–173.

Harel, J., Kaplan, H., Avimeir-Patt, R., & Ben-Aaron, M. (2006). The child's active role in mother-child, father-child psychotherapy: A psychodynamic approach to the treatment of relational disturbances. *Psychology and Psychotherapy: Theory, Research and Practice*, 79(1), 23–36.

Kaplan, H., Harel, Y., & Avimeir-Patt, R. (2010). *Parent-child psychotherapy: An encounter between the therapeutic act and theory*. Haifa: University of Haifa. (In Hebrew).

Kramer, E. (1958). *Art therapy in a children's community*. Springfield, IL: Charles C. Thomas.

Kris, E. (1952). *Psychoanalytic explorations in art*. New York, NY: International Universities Press.

Luria, L. (2002). Tension in play: In Winnicott's footsteps. In E. Perroni (Ed.), *Play: Psychoanalysis and other disciplines* (pp. 88–103). Tel Aviv: Yediot Aharonot. (In Hebrew).

Mahler, M. S., Pine, F., & Bergman, A. (1975). *The psychological birth of the human infant*. New York, NY: Basic Books.

Markman-Zinemanas, D. (2011). The additional value of art psychotherapy: Visual symbolization. *Academic Journal of Creative Art Therapies*, 2, 131–139.

Moon, C. (2010). *Materials and media in art therapy: Critical understandings of diverse artistic vocabularies*. New York, NY: Routledge.

Naumburg, M. (1966). *Dynamically oriented art therapy: Its principles and practices*. New York, NY and London: Grune & Stratton/Chicago, IL: Magnolia Street.

Shapira, G. (2005). Destruction as raw material for creating. In H. Davyash (Ed.), *Adolescence and injury*. Jerusalem: The Summit Institute. (In Hebrew).

Snir, S., & Hazut, T. (2012). Observing the relationship: Couple patterns reflected in joint paintings. *The Arts in Psychotherapy*, 39, 11–18.

Snir, S., & Regev, D. (2013) ABI: Art-based intervention questionnaire. *The Arts in Psychotherapy*, 40, 338–346.

Snir, S., & Wiseman, H. (2010). Attachment in romantic couples and perceptions of a joint drawing session. *The Family Journal*, 18(2), 116–126.

6 Working with Parents in the Parent-Child Art Psychotherapy Framework

In the previous chapter, we discussed art therapists' various roles within the parent-child psychotherapy model. This chapter focuses on working with parents, their attitudes toward parent-child art psychotherapy, ways of engaging and involving parents in therapy to achieve more beneficial therapeutic outcomes, and specific intervention techniques.

Parents' Attitudes Toward Their Involvement in Parent-Child Art Psychotherapy

Most parents take part in parent-child art psychotherapy with an open mind and a willingness to learn and improve their relationships with their children. According to most therapists, the active participation of parents is a significant factor in decreasing concerns having to do with criticism of their parenting abilities or competition over the child's affections (Kaplan, Harel, & Avimeir-Patt, 2010). These parents, who engage in therapeutic work with a sense of commitment and a desire for change, often successfully create a different daily reality for themselves and their children. Despite the complex nature of the situation, therapists feel that parents can be mobilized to be involved in therapeutic work and become agents of change that help make a real difference in their child's life. According to most therapists, the driving force behind their participation in parent-child psychotherapy is their central and fundamental role as parents, and their desire to be good ones. On the other hand, most therapists emphasize the complexities involved in the parental role. Working with a child in distress is a delicate issue in which parents often feel their competencies are being tested. At the start of the therapeutic process, most parents fear the watchful eye of the therapist (Kaplan et al., 2010). In many interviews, the therapists stated that this situation requires a great deal of strength and perseverance. Many parents experience a wide range of emotions, ranging from fear and concern for their child, to feelings of guilt about failing as a parent when dealing with the problems that brought the child to therapy. The literature also discusses the parents' feelings when working in this setting (Ishai & Oren, 2006). A significant number of therapists also referred to the conflictual nature of the parental role when engaging in the parent-child art psychotherapy process, and the difficulties and fears parents face at this stage. One therapist (Regev & Snir, 2014) reported that she feels that parents often attend therapy from a place of great distress. They describe their hardships but tend to reject suggested methods of intervention, claiming these techniques have been tried and failed. They ask for help, but in fact they come to therapy to show that nothing helps. Thus, parental willingness may also be mixed with rivalry, expressed initially through competition over who knows more (and best) for the child.

How to Recruit Parents to Participate in the Parent-Child Art Psychotherapy Process

The prime issue at the start of the therapy process is the best way to integrate the parents, despite these obstacles. Many therapists indicated they were preoccupied with this problem. Several approaches emerged from the interviews and the authors' own extensive experience, as described below.

Listening to the Parents

All the therapists felt that listening to the parents is a powerful tool to keep parents in the therapeutic loop and enable them to benefit from it. Listening to the parents affirms the importance of their knowledge of themselves, and the child, and helps the therapist understand the bigger picture outside of the therapy room. All the therapists considered that listening strengthens the alliance between the therapist and the parent and makes them partners in the therapeutic journey, but also serves as a container that holds and supports the parents. When the therapist meets with the parents, the parents describe their child's condition, including what happens at home and at school, and how they experience the child's condition in relation to the goals of therapy. The assumption is that the parents know their child better and more thoroughly than anyone else, and all the information they provide is significant for the therapist. Bion's (1967) notion of "container" is defined as an experience in the client's mind in which a segment of the fantasized self is relocated (contained) to the therapist, who in some way translates this event into a real experience for him or her. For this reason, Bion suggested that the therapist should come to every therapy session "without memory and without desire." This objective can also help the parent-child therapist to be available to genuinely listen to the parents, try to experience the way in which they experience their children, and thus also learn a great deal about the child. It can also help encourage the parents to engage in therapeutic work and explore the feelings they bring with them and the reasons that led them to seek therapy for their child.

Refraining from Judging the Parents

All the therapists strongly concurred that when parents start the therapeutic process, they become exposed and vulnerable. This vulnerability can be aggravated when parents feel weakness and guilt when appealing for help. Most therapists agreed that this is the reason why most parents have a need to feel safe in therapy. A sense of security can lead to the development of a safe relationship between therapist and client, and between spouses. Previous studies have suggested that the creation of a safe relationship between the child, the parents, and the therapist contributes to the development of the reflective function, which is also one of the objectives of parent-child art psychotherapy (Fonagy & Target, 1997). The therapists were unanimous in stressing the importance of adopting a non-judgmental stance with parents, since this helps engage parents in the therapeutic process. In the first intake session, therapists tell the parents that they are aware that attending parent-child art psychotherapy with their children is not easy and that they may occasionally feel threatened, but it is important to them as therapists to make it clear that they are not going to be judged.

Highlighting the Child's Positive Qualities

Many therapists addressed the need to highlight the child's positive qualities as a way to help parents play an active role in the therapeutic process. This stance, which views hope and optimism as key elements in therapy, is supported extensively by research and the theoretical literature (e.g., Frank & Frank, 1991; Irving et al., 2004). By pinpointing the child's positive qualities and character traits, the therapist transfers a positive image of the child to the parent. This attitude may be contrary to previous feedback the parents have received from external sources regarding the child and the child's behavior. However, this process enables the parent and the therapist to associate and cooperate in shared admiration of the child's good qualities, which enhances their parenting capacity and strengthens the alliance between parent and therapist. One therapist described a child with ADHD, learning disabilities, and slow speech. During therapy, the parents focused on the child's difficulties, but as therapy progressed, they discovered his abilities, including the fact that he played games very intelligently and was also very creative. The therapist made sure to discuss this issue thoroughly with the parents, which enabled them to see their child in a different way.

Intervention Techniques in Parent Training Sessions

The next section specifically addresses parent training and how these sessions unfold. We focus on key intervention techniques implemented by art therapists when they meet with parents for training during parent-child art psychotherapy.

Observing the Parent-Child Sessions

The first stage of the parent training sessions, according to all the therapists, deals with observations of parent-child interactions during therapy. Together with the therapist, the parents examine the artworks created during the alternating individual parent-child therapy sessions and try to reconstruct the feelings that arose during these sessions and specify what they can learn from this joint observation. The therapists emphasized the importance of the parents' explanations of how they felt during the sessions. However, they also described themselves as active partners in the observation process, who enabled the parents to establish and understand connections between the themes that emerged in the drawings and events that occur in the child's life. The presence of an artistic product that acts as a record and testimony of the therapy session plays an important and unique role in the parent training sessions in parent-child art psychotherapy. Malchiodi (2007) argued that the language of art, which combines colors, shapes, lines, and images, serves as a vehicle for expression when words are no longer present. This therapeutic field uses the nonverbal language of art for growth, insight, and personal transformation, as well as a means of communication of thoughts, feelings, and perceptions having to do with external realities and life experiences. The interviews suggested that the artistic product that was created during the parent-child art therapy session is used and observed during parent training sessions and serves as a mirror, or form of documentation of the previous parent-child interactions. The observation of this art work helps parents perceive the changes that have occurred during therapy. One of the therapists stated that even in difficult cases when parents find it hard to see the struggles or to observe the changes that have occurred as a result of therapy, observation of drawings can be very effective and meaningful. She described the case of a father and child who attended therapy together. They created a joint painting where the father primarily used two colors. During the joint observation process, the child said to his father: "You see, even when you're drawing with me, you're busy with your work . . . These are the colors of your logo and they take over our lives and also take over our drawing . . ." This issue was further discussed during parental training, which enabled the father to better understand his presence with his son.

Comparing What Transpires in the Therapy Room and What Occurs at Home

Most therapists discussed the crucial issue of comparisons between events in the therapy room and similar events at home. As part of the parent-child psychotherapy framework, and much like group therapy (Yalom, 1995), patterns of relationships can be seen to develop between the dyad partners in a way that allows for the formation of a relatively rapid connection between insights gained in therapy and their implementation in real life outside the therapy room. The therapists considered that these comparisons helped parents to identify repetitive interaction patterns and think together as partners about the role they play during such interactions. One of the therapists described talking to a mother in parent training: "You say that he has anger outbursts and I want to see when it happens, what transpired in these cases." If the therapist can view the same situation as it occurs inside and outside the therapy room, it should be possible to think of feasible solutions together with the parents. The therapist's position should be humble and approachable, with the understanding that the only way to grasp the bigger picture is to work together.

Parental Guidance (on a Practical Level)

The art therapists stated that they tend to help parents on a practical level during the training sessions, particularly when dealing with interactions with the child and developmental issues. For example, one of the therapists mentioned that she often describes what is appropriate or inappropriate for a particular family in terms of the child's age. She tells them about the developmental stage, what this means in relation to separation and independence, and what can be done at home to implement this information. The therapists described a number of specific issues that require practical guidance when meeting with parents. The first has to do with areas in which the parents are less involved in the child's life. For example, therapists mentioned the importance of playing together and how this impacts the child's development. The second issue concerns the relationship between the parents and other adults. For example, this can involve helping parents strengthen their relationship with their child's teacher. The third is the dilemmas faced by parents when deciding how to behave in certain situations in front of the child, specifically regarding behavioral problems and boundary issues. Kaplan and colleagues (Kaplan et al., 2010) argued that providing parents with a "psychological education" is one of the therapist's primary roles. The aim is to help parents attend to their interpretations, in particular those related to expectations that are unrealistic given the child's age, or opinions regarding what is normal or abnormal in the child's behavior or in their relationship. However, there were differences in the ways that the therapists dealt with parents in therapy. Many said that they prepared for parent training sessions by drawing on their own experience. A few therapists noted that they often refer parents to other sources of information and give examples from their personal lives. For example, they described how they acted when encountering a similar problem with their own children.

An Appraisal of the Parent's Emotional State

The art therapists related to the therapeutic aspects that take place within the framework of parent training that touch on issues and representations that are related to the parents. This approach, which was discussed in Chapter 1, is based on the assumption that the way a parent responds to a child is often affected by internal working models emerging through the parent's own early interactions with key caretakers. There are a number of theorists who describe parental internal content as the driving force behind parents' understanding of their child, which may also influence attachment patterns with the child as an infant. The relationship between parent and infant is affected by a comprehensive world of internal projections (Fraiberg, Adelson, & Shapiro, 1975; Lieberman, Padro, Van Horn, & Harris, 2005; Manzano, Palacio-Espesa, & Zilka, 2005). Processing this content plays a central role in parent training sessions in parent-child psychotherapy. One of the therapists described her work with a father of a girl with ADHD. It became clear that the father had a complex relationship with his daughter because she reminded him of his sister, and he feared that she was becoming like her.

Many therapists emphasized the importance of their shared journey with parents during therapy, and their willingness to proceed on a journey of self-discovery with them. Parents attend parent-child psychotherapy to help their child, but in the process they encounter their own self, their parenting styles, and also become familiar with their own strengths, weaknesses, problems, and discomfort. Many therapists pointed out that when parents choose to address emotional issues related to themselves, the therapist will try to connect the content to parenthood and the relationship with the child in therapy. One of the therapists described a mother who attended therapy with her daughter. The father was often not home and the mother was dealing with many fears and had trouble sleeping at night. As part of parent training, the therapist talked to the mother about her fears and the impact of these fears on her daughter.

Addressing Issues within a Couple's Relationship

Many therapists reported that they often address issues relating to the parents' relationship in parent training sessions. They noted that many parents who are experiencing marital issues refuse to attend couples therapy but consent to taking part in parent-child psychotherapy to help their child. During therapy, many issues that emerge in the parental relationship often have an impact on parenting styles and children's functioning. Occasionally, marital issues can create stagnation in the therapeutic process. Most therapists stated that when parents introduce complex issues from their relationship into the parent training conversation, they appear to be primarily engaged in a struggle between one another, and the therapist will refer them to marital counseling held at the same time as parent-child psychotherapy. During parent-child psychotherapy, most therapists attempt to encourage parents to support each other, and highlighted the importance of the co-parenting relationship, which should be geared toward favoring the development of their child (Fivaz-Depeursinge & Corboz-Warney, 1999).

One of the therapists described a couple who came to therapy with their 4-year-old daughter. The parents felt that the child demanded all of their attention and energy, to the extent that they had nothing left for their other daughter or for themselves. During the parent training sessions, it became clear that the mother did not trust the father with the children and felt the need to be present at all times. The constant presence of the mother did not allow the father to develop his own relationship with his daughters. These parents were referred to marital counseling to help them examine their issues of trust.

Envy and Jealousy of the Therapist

Some therapists addressed the issues of jealousy that arise during parent-child psychotherapy. Jealousy is often expressed toward the therapist and what he or she represents in the relationship, including the therapist's ability to communicate with the child, to contain feelings, and so on. While some therapists chose to ignore situations where they identified jealousy in the therapy room or felt that a parent was competing with them, others argued that due to the immense presence of competitiveness during therapy, they preferred to work on it rather than ignore it. One therapist described an instance where a mother brought a cake to nearly every session of parent-child art psychotherapy, and at some point the therapist felt that this affected their interactions. She realized that the mother was trying to prove to her that she was a good mother. They discussed the issue during the parent training session in an attempt to help the mother perceive and recognize that side of herself.

Using Art During Parent Training Sessions

Most therapists mentioned that they occasionally use art during parent training (Shamri-Zeevi, Regev, & Snir, 2015) as another way to access internal content and issues that are not being verbally addressed, issues that the parents are not fully aware of, or that are otherwise hard to reach. One of the therapists discussed her first experience with this issue: "I had a session with these parents a month ago, and I finished the sessions and I was sweating, I felt as if I was digging into a stone, I couldn't make any progress with them. And last week, just a few minutes before they arrived, I said to myself: I can't do this again, and I decided to let them draw. At first, they were very frightened, they didn't understand what I wanted from them, but gradually, they were able to draw and I felt that it was great."

The use of art in the training sessions follows the same guidelines of using art in therapy as a non-verbal method of expression and as a way to cope with internal content (Betensky, 1995). Many therapists stated that beyond reaching into unconscious content, the use of art also helped parents engage in mentalization. According to Gavron (2010), creating and observing art triggers processes of "metaphorical insight" (Wix, 1997), and this turns art into a meaningful tool that not only depicts and represents content, but also promotes significant internal insights in the participants. Using art appears to enable parents to access parts of themselves that they are less aware of, and develop mental processes that help them look at themselves and their relationship with their child.

Some therapists stated that the use of art during parent training sessions was not appropriate for either them or for the parents because the language of art is often not an obvious choice for self-expression on the part of the parents, and may make them feel that they have partially relinquished control over the situation. On the one hand, parents often shy away from art-making because many of them have not engaged with art materials for many years and at times perceive this medium as restricted to use with children. In addition, working with art requires longer parent training sessions to create a balance between the creative part and the verbal part where parents express their dominant concerns (Shamri-Zeevi et al., 2015). On the other hand, when working with art materials, it is harder for parents to control the product and block significant content from surfacing, and it is often possible to use the artistic process and the observation of the art product to learn something significant about their inner world. One of the therapists described her work with art during a parent training session with a father who strongly opposed therapy because he claimed that his daughter had no problems to begin with. During the intake session, he was asked to draw his family and was surprised to see that he drew his oldest daughter to be much younger than his youngest son. This drawing helped him focus his own feelings and the reasons why he perceived his daughter as so young.

Therapists use several art-based intervention techniques with parents. The first taps the representation of the parent, the child, and the relationship between them. For example: "I ask them to draw any family activity. And then I see the dynamics of the relationship. For example, a mother drew the whole family watching TV and playing together, but the mother had her back to them. We then talked about the issue of detachment and distance or how close she feels to her family, and many issues surfaced in the conversation." Alternatively: "I can ask parents to draw a shape that represents themselves and their child." Or: "I can ask the parents to draw the timeline of their birth, and to draw themselves from the moment they were born to today, using only a pencil line. Afterwards, I ask them to draw the same line for their children. Some parents draw their own lines and then they draw an identical line for their children. They do not see themselves as separate from their children." Another technique consists of asking the parents to make an artistic response to what the child created in therapy. The parent can respond to a child's artwork freely or construct something in relation to the work. For instance, a parent might draw a window and then choose where to put the window on the child's artwork. This can lead to discussions about the parent's choice of work and the artwork itself.

Summary

- Most parents attend parent-child art psychotherapy with an open mind and a desire to improve their relationship with their children.
- The therapeutic setting is not easy for parents, but most therapists feel that their presence is a catalyst for change.
- A therapist who is non-judgmental, who listens to parents, and highlights the positive aspects of a child's behavior can help recruit and encourage parents to participate in the therapeutic process.
- The parent training framework within the parent-child psychotherapy model helps parents create change. The therapists did not all agree on specific work methods (whether to refer the parents to further sources of information, whether to address issues of jealousy, etc.). Most therapists employed a variety of methods, including asking parents and children to work with the art materials, and these therapists also indicated that art-making made a significant contribution to building their relationship.
- Engaging in art-based interventions can be helpful in parent training; however, they are not always appropriate for all therapists or parents.

References

Betensky, M. G. (1995). *What do you see? Phenomenology of therapeutic art expression*. London: Jessica Kingsley.

Bion, W. (1967). Notes on memory and desire. In E. Bott-Spillius (Ed.), *Melanie Klein today* (Vol. 2, pp. 17–21). London: Routledge.

Fivaz-Depeursinge, E., & Corboz-Warney, A. (1999). *The primary triangle*. New York, NY: Basic Books.

Fonagy, P., & Target, M. (1997). Attachment and reflective function: Their role in self organization. *Development and Psychopathology, 9*, 679–900.

Fraiberg, S., Adelson, E., & Shapiro, V. (1975). Ghost in the nursery: A psychoanalytic approach to the problems of impaired infant-mother relationships. *Journal of the American Academy of Child Psychiatry, 14*, 387–421.

Frank, J. D., & Frank, J. B. (1991). *Persuasion and healing*. Baltimore, MD: Johns Hopkins University Press.

Gavron, T. (2010). Psychotherapy and assessment of parent-child relationship through joint painting. In H. Kaplan, J. Harel, & R. Pat-Avimeir (Eds.), *Parent-child psychotherapy* (pp. 390–414). Haifa: University of Haifa. (In Hebrew).

Irving, L. M., Snyder, C. R., Cheavens, J., Gravel, L., Hanke, J., Hilberg, P., & Nelson, N. (2004). The relationships between hope and outcomes at the pre-treatment, beginning, and later phases of psychotherapy. *Journal of Psychotherapy Integration, 14*(4), 419–443.

Ishai, R., & Oren, D. (2006). Blocked parenthood and fulfilled parenthood: Parenting as creation and about the contribution of dynamic psychoanalytic parent guidance. *Sihot-Dialogue: Israel Journal of Psychotherapy, 20*(3), 251–264. (In Hebrew).

Kaplan, H., Harel, Y., & Avimeir-Patt, R. (2010). *Parent-child psychotherapy: An encounter between the therapeutic act and theory.* Department of Psychology, University of Haifa. (In Hebrew).

Lieberman, A. F., Padro, E., Van Horn, P., & Harris, W. W. (2005). Angels in the nursery: The intergenerational transmission of benevolent parental influences. *Infant Mental Health Journal, 26*(6), 504–520.

Malchiodi, C. A. (2007). *The art therapy sourcebook.* New York, NY: McGraw-Hill.

Manzano, G., Palacio-Espesa, P., & Zilka, N. (2005). *Narcissistic scenarios of parenting: The clinic for parenting consultation.* Tel Aviv: Tola'at Sefarim. (In Hebrew).

Regev, D., & Snir, S. (2014). Working with parent-child art psychotherapy. *The Arts in Psychotherapy, 41*(5), 511–518.

Shamri-Zeevi, L., Regev, D., & Snir, S. (2015). The usage of art materials in the framework of parental training. *The Arts in Psychotherapy, 45,* 56–63.

Wix, L. (1997). Picturing the relationship: An image-focused case study of a daughter and her mother. *American Journal of Art Therapy, 35*(3), 74–82.

Yalom, I. D. (1995). *The theory and practice of group psychotherapy.* New York, NY: Basic Books.

7 Unique Challenges in the Parent-Child Art Psychotherapy Model

Art therapists face a specific range of difficulties when they choose to work according to the parent-child art psychotherapy model. The first section of this chapter addresses general problems in the work setting, and the second deals with problems specifically applicable to art therapists.

General Difficulties

Technical Difficulties Related to Parental Presence

Some therapists addressed the technical difficulties that affect the parent-child therapeutic setting and work process. These difficulties are related to the presence and active participation of the parents in the therapeutic process. Parental participation in the parent-child art psychotherapy model is not easy for families, particularly when parents have additional children. The parents may initially appear eager to engage in the therapeutic process, but with time, and often as forms of resistance develop, and unexpectedly the difficulties in therapy become more complex, parents may find it harder to rearrange their schedules so that one of them can attend and be part of the therapeutic process. One therapist described a family that at the outset seemed to be very committed to the therapeutic process, but with time the father found it difficult to leave work on time and the mother was not always able to attend therapy with their son. This created a situation in which any excuse, whether it was a social event, a party, or bad weather, was used to cancel the therapy session. Some therapists emphasized that it was particularly hard for working parents to take part in the therapeutic process, especially when they were the breadwinners in the family.

It can also be challenging to arrange meetings with parents every three weeks, in addition to the therapy sessions with the children. In a private setting, this places additional burdens on the parents in terms of time and money. In the public sphere, these additional sessions may be hard to schedule and may not occur at all. For these reasons, the parent training sessions often take place instead of the sessions with the child. In addition, a study (Shamri-Zeevi, Regev, & Snir, 2015) showed that when the parents choose to use art materials during parent training sessions, a regular 45- to 50-minute session is not long enough, and the therapists have to extend it.

Difficulties with Art Materials

Some therapists mentioned that parents are often uninterested or unwilling to work with art materials. This may be because most have not worked with art materials for years and may feel that they are more suitable for children. These parents may attend therapy with their children, but tend to sit at a distance, which makes it difficult to include them in joint work. One of the therapists mentioned dealing with parents who said: "Listen, this isn't for me, I can't bear it, it upsets me, what is this nonsense?"

Difficulties Regarding the Parents' Skills and General Abilities

A few therapists mentioned situations in which the parents are willing to take part in parent-child art psychotherapy, but whose mental abilities may not be sufficient for this type of therapy: "Sometimes when there is a parent with limited abilities, or one who had a very difficult childhood or difficult experiences in life, it can be very hard."

Factors Hindering the Therapeutic Process

Some therapists noted that individual differences can make joint work in therapy complicated. As is the case in group therapy, differences between clients can be considerable. Parents and children may each work at a different pace, such that when one finishes working, the other may have barely started. Clients also vary in the extent to which they object to getting their hands dirty. A child who is on the verge of a significant emotional work process with art materials may be hampered because the parent is constantly concerned about keeping the child clean. The pace of therapy can also vary. A parent and child who were in a symbiotic relationship may find that one has experienced a form of change and wants more independence, whereas the other still needs a close, dependent relationship. Clients have different personalities, dispositions, and behavior (e.g., the parent or child may be energetic and dynamic, while the other is quiet and preoccupied). One therapist addressed this issue: "You need to be there with two people who have different needs and desires, and you have to be there for both of them, and not only for one of them." In such cases, the therapist needs to be very creative in finding a "middle ground" between parent and child; working together on this issue may constitute a crucial part of therapy, and essentially mirror their difficulties in reality.

The Challenge of Focusing on the Child as the Client in Therapy

Parents who attend parent-child art psychotherapy are individuals, as well as partners and parents of at least one child. Often it can be challenging to direct their attention to the child and away from other areas of their lives. In these cases, the therapeutic spotlight may shift to other personal issues in the parents' lives such as marital problems or problems with their other children. One therapist described a situation where after a year of therapy and significant improvement in the condition of the child in therapy, the parents began to raise issues that they had with their other child during the parent training sessions. It was clear that they found it difficult to part from the holding therapeutic environment and tried to use this setting to deal with other issues that were bothering them. The therapist re-established the child as the central focus in therapy and referred the parents to a different and more suitable form of therapy to deal with their other child. In another case, a divorced mother brought her daughter in for therapy because she had experienced tensions between her own parents. The mother tried to use the parent training sessions to process her own experiences concerning the divorce and found it hard to make time to think about her child.

Difficulties That Are Exclusive to Therapists

The Therapist's Ability to Provide a Holding Environment

Being a parent-child art therapist is a complex task that requires great ability for containment. The difficulties are manifold. Because there is more than one client in the room, the art therapist needs to find a way to suggest art materials and be sensitive to the needs of both clients simultaneously. Therapists also need to be trained in both child and adult therapy, since parent and child are both present in the room. The relationship between the parent and the child is also a factor, and the therapist needs to be skilled in the theories and working models that deal with relationships. One therapist touched on this issue: "It requires the therapist to be really focused and reflect the interaction, and constantly think about what happens to the child and what happens to the parent. It makes you grow." A number of therapists mentioned that many sensitive issues related to parenting emerge during therapy: "You need to be in a position and space that is very organized, because this type of therapy really stimulates you emotionally. It isn't so easy to maintain the therapeutic presence." The presence of a parent watching and observing the therapist during therapy can also cause anxiety: "When I was younger, I would get very anxious because I was under scrutiny by an adult in the room."

Refraining from Taking the Place of the Parents

Several therapists referred to specific difficulties related to their capacity to serving both the child and the parents without substituting for the parents or assuming their role, but rather by empowering parental competence. One therapist described a situation in which a child got angry and yelled in the therapy room, and it was clear that this behavior had to be stopped before the child damaged something in the room and possibly harmed himself and others. The therapist felt that she had to control the situation herself, but then realized how much more meaningful it would be if the parent confronted the child instead of sitting in the corner and watching the therapist handle the situation. In this situation, the therapist reflected the turn of events back to the parent and helped the parent take an active role in dealing with the child's behavior. During the parent training session after the therapy session, the parents and therapist were able to examine the situation more closely and gain insights in a way that was helpful if similar occurrences arose in the future.

The Parenting Style of the Parent-Child Art Therapist

The literature has dealt extensively with the issues of parenting and whether therapists who are not parents should engage in this kind of therapy. In *Motherhood: Psychoanalysis and Other Disciplines*, Emilia Perroni (2009) deals with the difference between the concept of motherhood and the concept of motherliness, a distinction first drawn by psychoanalyst Helene Deutsch in 1964. The term motherhood describes the woman as a mother, and the term motherliness is a personality trait that expresses an emotional stance toward others and oneself, regardless of the connection to biological motherhood. Thus, therapists who are not parents may have the essential qualities to express appropriate emotional attitudes toward others and toward themselves. The therapists we interviewed referred to their own parenting and how their status as being or not being a parent is reflected in their work. Similarly, many students studying parent-child art psychotherapy are concerned about whether they will be able to handle this therapeutic approach and work so closely with parents when they are not parents themselves. Opinions on this issue were varied among the therapists we interviewed, which further indicates its complexity. Some therapists believed that clients can be treated through the parent-child art psychotherapy model even if the therapist is not a parent. Qualities such as empathy and the ability to understand the experience of parenting that these therapists experienced as children can help therapists better understand the parents' position without having experienced it themselves. The therapists also gave examples of parent-child art therapists who were not mothers, but worked as professionals in the field. Some therapists felt that being a parent enriches the therapeutic work because parenting is a unique experience that leads to new feelings and a better understanding of one's own parenthood. Only a few therapists felt that being a parent was a critical factor before engaging in the parent-child psychotherapy model.

There are several ways in which the status of parenthood of the parent-child psychotherapist can enhance and enrich therapy. A significant number of therapists mentioned that being parents helped them feel more empathy toward the parents of their clients: "I think that being a parent contributes another layer to your internal dialogue, because we often do not share our relationship with our children, but it gives the therapist an additional internal aspect that makes you more empathetic because of the similar experiences that you had with your children." The second feature relates to knowledge. Most therapists clearly stated that being a parent enhanced and broadened what they knew about raising children and facilitated their relationship with parents in therapy. Some therapists commented that occasionally, in certain situations, and after much thought, they shared their experiences as parents with the child's parents. One of the therapists mentioned that her experience as a mother of a child with special needs helped her understand the position of parents in a variety of situations.

Despite the many benefits of being both a therapist and a parent, there are drawbacks as well. One relates to countertransference toward the parents in therapy. Kaplan, Harel, and Avimeir-Patt (2010) refer to a "parent" as having a role with many aspects, projections, and strengths, as well as processes of transference toward the "child," the "dyad couple," and the relationship between the parents. The therapist's feelings of countertransference can lead to a variety of complex emotions, which can complicate and impede the therapeutic process and the therapeutic alliance formed with the parent. The first has to do with issues of identification. There are certain situations where therapists identify with the parents in therapy. Some therapists argued that because they are parents themselves, they often find it easier to identify with the parents, which can damage the relationship and the therapeutic alliance with the child client. Occasionally, a child in therapy also reminds therapists of one of their children in one way or another, reinforcing the sense of identification with the parents.

The second relates to issues of judgment. Some therapists suggested that their own position as parents may at times cloud their ability to empathize with parents in therapy: "Often it's hard when you see parents who can't really see their own child. No matter what happens, they cannot see the child. Or all kinds of things that a parent may say or do that are not exactly what you do, you have another way of doing things."

The third relates to issues of jealousy. Approximately half of the therapists referred to the jealousy that they often feel toward parents who come to them for therapy. This jealousy stems from their acknowledgment of the parents' abilities or from the different situations that the parent is exposed to during therapy. One of the therapists described a situation in which a father was able to sit with his daughter on the carpet and could easily enter her world of imagination. Suddenly, the therapist felt both jealous and guilty for not engaging in the same activity with her own children.

Finally, while the therapist as a parent influences the relationship with the client, the therapist's parenting style may also be influenced by the clients. It is unquestionable that while observing a parent-child interaction, the therapist (as a parent) experiences a wide range of emotions. Some therapists referred to the impact of their work on their parenthood, in particular by underscoring the importance of joint quality time that enables playful interactions: "I can say that my eldest daughter was affected from the moment I started working with the parent-child psychotherapy model. Once or twice a week, I take my little girl to her grandmother's house and we don't go out, we close the door to her playroom and play there for half an hour. I'm now aware that parents often pay good money to close the door, sit in the room, and see their children."

Summary

- Therapists need to deal with a number of difficulties specific to the parent-child art psychotherapy model. The technical difficulties include the parents' ability to make time to come with their child every week and often also attend an additional parent training session. Parents may also find it hard to take part in creative processes together with their children, and may not be mentally equipped for this type of therapy. Parents and children may have considerable individual differences that can impede the process, and some parents find it difficult to focus solely on the child in therapy.
- Therapists also face a number of specific challenges. They must contain both clients, refrain from being the parent in therapy, and deal with the complex countertransference process that can take place when the therapists are parents themselves.

References

Kaplan, H., Harel, Y., & Avimeir-Patt, R. (2010). *Parent-child psychotherapy: An encounter between the therapeutic act and theory*. Haifa: University of Haifa. (In Hebrew).

Perroni, E. (Ed.). (2009). *Motherhood: Psychoanalysis and other disciplines*. The Van Leer Jerusalem Institute. Tel Aviv: Hakibbutz Hameuchad. (In Hebrew).

Shamri-Zeevi, L., Regev, D., & Snir, S. (2015). The usage of art materials in the framework of parental training. *The Arts in Psychotherapy*, 45, 56–63.

8 The Observation of Joint Paintings

The final five chapters of this book present a set of structured techniques for creating joint paintings that are suitable for parent-child art psychotherapy. The techniques differ in terms of their emphasis on the subject of the painting, the presence of abstract forms, the physical distance between the two creators, the transitions between togetherness and separation in the painting, the degree of playfulness, the presence of movement in the painting, the materials, and other features.

Before these techniques are presented, we provide some general information on the assessment of joint paintings. These insights are the outcome of our many years of clinical work but are also based on two research projects on the assessment of freely created joint paintings (paintings produced without specific instructions). The first research paper, Dr. Sharon Snir's dissertation, examined joint paintings created by couples (Snir & Hazut, 2012, 2013; Snir & Wiseman, 2010, 2013, 2015, 2016), and the second paper, a thesis written by Elizabeth Yakovson (Yakovson, 2014) for which we both served as academic supervisors, examined the joint paintings of mothers and their children in the latency stage. Despite the many differences between the joint paintings of adult couples and those of mothers and their children, the criteria for examining the paintings for assessment purposes are very similar. These criteria are described in our work as "pictorial phenomena" and are defined by the phenomenological approach to art therapy. Although these criteria have been defined in reference to unstructured paintings, they also help understand structured joint paintings.

Pictorial Phenomena

The term "pictorial phenomena" refers to the significant behaviors that emerge during the different stages of the creative process, as well as the characteristics of the final product. According to the phenomenological approach to art therapy, identifying and defining pictorial phenomena is an integral part of the process of assessment and therapy. The pictorial phenomena that become noticeable during the creative process serve as a vehicle to understanding the creator's experience, and help make hidden and unconscious content accessible for processing (Snir & Hazut, 2012).

When analyzing artwork, the phenomenological approach directs the observer to pictorial phenomena such as the type and size of the work format, the materials and tools, how they were used and how the work unfolded, the variety of colors that were used, the characteristics of the colors and shapes that fill the painting space, the chronological order in which they were chosen, their significance, and the relationships between them. The notion of pictorial phenomena also covers the issues that the client deals with during therapy, the efficiency of the artwork, the organization and planning of the artwork, and so on (Betensky, 1995). All of these elements convey information about the creator's inner world. Nevertheless, understanding the meaning of pictorial phenomena and the information that they reveal about the inner world of the creator is complex and not unequivocal. Even more than words and the spoken language, the artistic language can express different content in different circumstances. For example, a commonplace pictorial phenomenon such as the use of black paint on a page may occasionally express the need to be visible, or a statement about being present, whereas in other situations it may express a negative feeling such as anger or depression. Therefore, we believe that the best way to explore the significance of a pictorial phenomenon is by examining and viewing it within the context of other phenomena in the painting. For example, the use of black on a large page applied in a fairly organized manner while applying a great deal of pressure to create a large image with a bold presence may imply that black was chosen to make a statement in the painting. On the other hand, when the presence of the color black is less dominant and appears on a smaller page, this color may represent negative feelings. Moreover, just as the act of making creative artwork reflects internal aspects of the creator, viewers of this artwork are influenced and shaped by their own internal worlds. Therefore, when viewing joint artwork created during parent-child art psychotherapy, the process of interpretation needs to be done jointly by the therapist and the parent-child dyad, or by the therapist and the parent. The therapist's primary role is to direct the clients to observe their pictorial phenomena, be in touch with their inner experiences, and permeable to their own interpretations of the work. In addition, in many cases, it is very helpful for therapists to discuss parent-child paintings in their own supervision sessions to get a second opinion about their significance and implications.

The Phenomenology of Joint Paintings

The phenomenology of joint paintings refers to the interactive phenomena between the two creators that take place during the act of painting, and which are apparent in the creative process, on the page, and in the final product.

The Organization of the Painting on the Page

Perhaps the key pictorial phenomenon in the phenomenology of a joint painting is the way in which the creators orient themselves to the sheet of paper and arrange the shared space. Typically, when two people are given one page to draw on together, the half of the page in front of each individual is theoretically associated with this particular individual. However, many clients use the page as a joint space and position themselves across the entire width of the page in order to draw together. In other words, on a "joint painting" scale, one end corresponds to joint paintings in which each creator uses only half of the space in front of him or her, thus forming two separate paintings on one page. The other end of the scale corresponds to paintings created together on the entire page. Between these two anchors, the division of the page varies, and typically emerges from disagreements about how the space should be organized.

Another pictorial phenomenon related to this topic is the degree of coherency in the joint artwork. Were the creators able to "tell their story together" coherently? Did they want to and were they able to draw one painting together that was characterized by uniformity of style, based on a clear and agreed-upon subject, or were there sections that were not connected to one another and did not form one joint message? The extent to which the creators are able "to tell a joint story" in a coherent manner is considered a key indicator of the level of attachment in contemporary adult relationships (Crowell & Owens, 1996). In contrast, and according to the same approach, an overload and a degree of ambivalence may express dependency and the need for control, which are both considered characteristics of anxious attachment. By contrast, dissociation or idealization in the painting may express avoidant attachment (Snir & Wiseman, 2016).

The distance between the two creators is also a significant indicator. In unstructured joint paintings, there are differences between parent-child dyads in terms of the distance that the two creators establish on the page. Often there are large distances on the page; this takes place when the creators position themselves on the opposite sides of the page. Alternatively, some creators draw in layers, by superimposing their painting over that of their partner. Importantly, there may be changes in distance as the artwork progresses. For example, two creators may start painting at opposite ends from each other and gradually move closer, or the opposite can occur— they start by painting a single joint image and gradually move away until they each find their own private space on the page.

Finally, the space that each creator occupies on the page also tells a story. The joint paintings differ in terms of the percentage of the area that each creator occupies in the joint space. The perception of the space occupied in the joint space on the page can shed light on the balance of power, control, and the presence of the two creators as individuals as well. The parent often allows the child to draw in the central section of the page to give the child center stage. In other situations that are less conducive to the child, the parent may take over the central section of the page. For example, in Yakovson's (2014) study, one of the mothers drew three tall structures that filled the entire right side of the page. The structures also determined the content of the painting, and weakened her son's attempts at expression since he tried to erase the small images that he had drawn at the bottom of the page when he realized that they did not correspond to his mother's content.

Contact between Each Creator's Marks on the Page

Another important interactive pictorial phenomenon is the extent of contact between the elements drawn by the creators. When both creators place themselves relatively close to each other on the page, some still avoid touching each other's artworks. Others seek contact with their partner's paintings. The degree of contact can range from complete absence of contact to situations of partial contact (e.g., by adding or coloring near the elements created by the partner). Contact can also be expressed in extreme situations by the presence of considerable intense contact achieved when working in layers on top of one another. Contact and closeness between two partners may be indicative of closeness and intimacy, but too much contact can express conflict, aggression, or dependence. As mentioned above, the pictorial context, as well as the creator's experiences, may help understand the meaning of the type of contact for the parent-child dyad. In Yakovson's (2014) study, one of the mothers drew a cat and a girl on the bottom part of the page, and her daughter drew the images that appeared at the top of the page—butterflies and a skyline. The images were created far from each other physically. During the observation process, the mother said: "There is a distance between us . . . It bothered me during the actual painting process that we did not integrate them . . ."

Creating a Separate Space in the Painting

Some clients, particularly children but occasionally parents, may need to define their own separate space in the painting. This behavior may reflect the ongoing process of the affirmation of autonomy and separation from the parent during different stages of child development. In paintings, this space can be created by painting a barrier or a boundary to define the individual painting space. Often the separation space is created by the physical gesture of placing a hand down on the page or hiding part of the page. Many times, this is apparently done unconsciously and the barrier image functions as part of the painting (e.g., a big tree that divides the page in two, a colorful rainbow that defines a private space, etc.). There are cases where one of the partners will create a few personal images that are unique and may symbolize a personal, private space. For example, in Yakovson's (2014) study, one of the children decided to work with images that were familiar and available to him: circus performers he had recently seen in a film. When asked about it, the mother said that he selected the images from his own personal world: "He chose the 'theme' of the painting.

He chose to go in the direction of something familiar. He drew a circus that he had just seen in a cartoon." In specific cases, one of the partners may create an image that is very unclear, making it difficult for the other partner to join in and contribute. In very rare cases, one of the partners may draw a line and declare that it defines the partner's space. When there is considerable effort to achieve separation in the painting, there can be a drive for a sense of togetherness that can take place when neither partner is attempting to take control. Yakovson (2014) described a situation in which one of the mothers worked hard to create a joint painting with a high degree of "togetherness," which, in turn, left minimal space for individual expression. This was reflected when the mother very clearly directed the child what and where to draw on the page. She "corrected" images that she thought were unsuitable, occasionally even taking the paint from her child's hands and painting with them herself. In response, the child showed increasing signs of frustration. This was reflected in tears, anger, and verbal arguments. The child also kept to himself and finally avoided working on the joint page entirely.

Creating a Connection between the Two Partners on the Page

Occasionally, and most often when the child, the parent, or both partners feel that there is too much distance on the page, they will add an element that connects their two sections. This can be done by adding an image that connects their two other images (e.g., by painting a path between two houses). Alternatively, an additional image that contains elements from both separate images can be drawn (e.g., a bowl containing two separate pieces of fruit that were painted earlier by each partner). This enhancement is usually more frequent on the part of parents. The nature of the connection created by the additional image, as well as the context in which it takes place, suggests whether they express the need to adjust the degree of closeness, or whether they serve as an expression of anxiety caused by abandonment and dependency.

Relating to the Partner's Images on the Page

The joint painting encourages clients to consider and respond to their partner and their partner's paintings in a nonverbal way. Frequently, partners switch locations on the page and add features to the other's image. This can include adding leaves to a tree, or windows to a house. When this addition fits the initial image, does not change its nature, and does not relate to any other excessive element that the partner created, it can be assumed that the additional element will be mutually accepted and form part of the collaborative section of the painting. These can also serve and be experienced as support and perhaps empowerment for the initial image (e.g., when a parent adds fruit to a tree that the child drew). There are also cases where one of the partners mimics the work of the other and creates a playful dialogue. At times, it seems that exaggerated additional elements in the painting may express the need for excessive protection, involvement, or dependency. This can be the case when a parent responds continuously and consistently to each image that was drawn by the child. In cases such as these, the same fruit that was added to a tree may be experienced as an attempt to gain control and impose solutions. In Yakovson's (2014) study, one of the mothers drew a sheep and her daughter added an enclosure. This may suggest that the daughter wanted to be involved and present in the mother's paintings. In the interview, the mother said that she experienced the addition of the enclosure as an attempt to create a sense of closeness and togetherness in the painting: "Here we were together, we each started on our own sides, but then she [the daughter] made the connection, she put my sheep in an enclosure, and here we actually made it together . . ."

The Creation of Collaboration

When two partners are given a shared space to work in, they often view this as an invitation to create a joint artwork, even if the instruction is not explicit. Therefore, many clients intuitively engage their partners in joint artwork (e.g., by painting a border around the page that makes it clear that the page is seen as a joint space, or by creating an image that is meaningful to both partners and will encourage them to make a joint painting). The way the suggestion to work together is made is significant because it can be viewed at times as a forcible attempt to take control of the situation. It depends on the manner and intensity in which the collaborative work unfolds, but primarily depends on the nature of the relationship. Sometimes when there is a form of dependency, a suggestion to work together that would typically be perceived as subtle and understated may be experienced as overbearing and depreciating. When there is an initial offer to either cooperate or not, many different reactions corresponding to different types of consent can be seen. One typical reaction is compliance. For example, in Yakovson's (2014) study, one of the girls drew the entrance gate to a zoo, and when the mother understood what it represented, she began to draw animals that belong in a zoo. A less common response is the refusal to work together and a preference to work independently in a separate section of the page.

Alternatively, partners occasionally feel uncomfortable about working together on the page because of a possible feeling of insecurity in the relationship regarding their ability to act independently in the presence of the other. During these situations, certain individuals will respond to the offer to draw together by creating a separate space for themselves in the painting. When invited to draw separately on the same page, some comply and draw separately (even against their will) beside their partners. A few people may find it difficult to acquire the need for separation, which is a key phase in child development, and try to find ways to work in a closed area of the page.

The Creator's Style of Work (Symbolism of Style)

Painting style refers to the person's "handwriting" while painting. Style can refer to the degree of realism or abstraction, the nature of the strokes, or where they fall on the continuum from faint to bold, light to heavy. An individual's painting style can indicate personal qualities, the level of sharing and cooperation or similarity between partners, and the extent to which the partners maintain different expressions in the joint work. The degree of compatibility between the partners' painting styles is also a key feature.

The selection of similar colors, similar images, and similar symbolism of style is often unconscious and may indicate mutual attentiveness and joint emotional and reflective inner worlds. Since it is expected that the parent will adapt to the child's needs, we also look at the parent's ability to adapt to the child's painting style. Some parents are able to recognize the disparities in the two painting styles and make the necessary changes during the painting process to adapt and accommodate the child. For example, when a mentally disabled adolescent and her mother were painting together, the mother was surprised when she noticed her daughter's motor difficulties and changed her painting style to better fit with that of her daughter.

Behavioral Traits During the Creative Process

The physical and verbal behavior that takes place during the painting process, both in relation to the artwork and between the partners, is also part of the phenomenology of joint painting. At times, the creative process is accompanied by laughter, which may indicate a good positive mood, or there may be slight confusion and difficulty in dealing with the shared creative process. Every so often, there are gestures such as a gentle pat or an affectionate touch, or aggressive physical movements such as pushing or putting a hand down in the center of the page. As part of the behavioral observation process, the degree of mobility is also examined, as well as levels of concentration and verbal communication that take place during the creative process.

The Subject Matter and the Features of the Images

A great deal of information about the relationship can be obtained by studying the subject and the images in the painting. Parent and child often select images that are meaningful to them both, such as a shared activity like bicycling or the family dog, and express their sense of togetherness in this way. From time to time, a subject is selected that is clearly solely related to the child. This includes characters from a story that the child likes or images related to the child's favorite hobby. In these situations, it often seems that the parent and the child have decided together to deal with the child's issues in therapy. At times, this may be linked to the inability to allow the parent to have space in the shared world (this is clearly dependent on other pictorial phenomena that appear simultaneously). In this case, the role of the therapist is to help create an appropriate space for the parent as a person in the relationship. The subject matter can contain frightening images, representing the more difficult parts of the experience for one or both of the partners, which can be addressed in the painting by both the parent and the child in terms of sublimation and other unconscious processes. There are also humorous images associated with the playful features of painting together. Frequently, the family can be drawn in a concrete way, or as a family of animals or family of trees. Sometimes the parent and child find their point of meeting in the subject of the painting. For example, in Yakovson's (2014) study, one child began to draw a rainbow and his mother added a sun and later helped him color the rainbow. Afterwards, the boy drew figures on the right side of the page that were standing on what appeared to be sand, and the mother drew the sea with fish on the top left side of the page. The subject matter allows the therapist to explore the world of representations of the parent and child. The family painting can reveal closeness, size, subgroups, location, and so on. The world of images can also show aggression in the relationship through the use of images of wild animals, sharp teeth, and so on. In this case, the therapist identifies who created the aggressive image, examines the meaning and context of the location of the image on the page, and attempts to link this to the relationship between the partners.

Summary

- *Pictorial phenomena*: The term "pictorial phenomena" refers to the significant behaviors that emerge during the different stages of the creative process, as well as the characteristics of the final product. According to the phenomenological approach to art therapy, the identification and definition of pictorial phenomena are an integral part of the process of assessment and therapy.
- *The phenomenology of joint paintings*: The phenomenology of joint paintings refers to the interactive phenomena between the two creators that take place during the act of painting, and are evident in the creative process, on the page, and in the final product. These include the organization of the painting on the page, the contact between each creator's marks on the page, creating a separate space in the painting, creating a connection between two partners on the page, relating to the partner's images on the page, the creation of collaborations, the creator's style of work (symbolism of style), behavioral traits during the creative process, and the subject matter and the characteristics of the images.

References

Betensky, M. (1995). *What do you see? Phenomenology of therapeutic art expression.* London: Jessica Kingsley.

Crowell, J. A., & Owens, G. (1996). *Current relationships interview and scoring system.* (Unpublished Manuscript). State University of New York at Stony Brook.

Snir, S., & Hazut, T. (2012). Observing the relationship: Couple patterns reflected in joint paintings. *The Arts in Psychotherapy, 39,* 11–18.

Snir, S., & Hazut, T. (2013). "To see the connection": Reflecting relationship patterns in joint drawings. *Conversations: The Israeli Psychotherapy Journal, 3,* 290–296. (In Hebrew).

Snir, S., & Wiseman, H. (2010). Attachment in romantic couples and perceptions of a joint drawing session. *The Family Journal, 18*(2), 116–126.

Snir, S., & Wiseman, H. (2013). Relationship patterns of connectedness and individuality in couples as expressed in the couple joint drawing method. *The Arts in Psychotherapy, 40,* 501–508.

Snir, S., & Wiseman, H. (2015). Joint drawing interpersonal recall in insecurely attached couples. *The Arts in Psychotherapy, 44,* 11–18.

Snir, S., & Wiseman, H. (2016). Couples' joint drawing patterns: Associations with self-report measures of interpersonal patterns and attachment styles. *The Arts in Psychotherapy, 48,* 28–37.

Yakovson, E. (2014). *Examining the main themes and pictorial phenomena that are reflected in the joint paintings of children and their mothers, as a central technique in parent-child psychotherapy.* (Unpublished Master's Dissertation). University of Haifa, Israel. (In Hebrew).

Part II

Intervention Techniques

9 Leadership Exercises

Introduction

The final five chapters of this book describe variants on the joint drawing task. These intervention exercises and techniques are based on the teachings of the late Mr. Peretz Hesse, in collaboration with Mrs. Tamar Hazut and Mrs. Judith Siano at the University of Haifa art therapy training program. Chapter 9 discusses a series of joint drawings aimed at strengthening and replacing the roles of leadership within the dyad. Chapter 10 discusses play activities that gradually promote the formation of a projective image that represents internal content and serves as a basis for exploration within the dyad. Chapter 11 presents exercises promoting the transition between being together to being alone, to enable alternations between intimacy and autonomy within the dyad. Chapter 12 describes different ways to encourage the dyad to engage in family representations via projective techniques. Chapter 13 illustrates joint drawing techniques that blur the boundaries between members of the dyad as they act as a single unit during the task. All are accompanied by examples and illustrations by parents and children who volunteered to experience the techniques for the purpose of this book accompanied by an art therapy student who served as the interviewer.

This chapter addresses leadership exercises through three intervention techniques: "the leader and the follower," "the chase," and "drawing in nine squares." These three all encourage the exchange of leadership roles within the dyad. During the exercises, one of the members in the dyad is the leader, and the other member is there to follow. After doing the task once, the positions are swapped, and the leader becomes the follower, and vice versa. These intervention techniques thus approach issues of control on many different levels. The first is as the leader (parent or child): what happens when I am in a position of power and control? Am I attentive to my partner's rhythm? Do I try to challenge him or her? Am I willing to accept his or her opinion? The second is the person being led (parent or child): do I trust my partner and allow myself to fall back on him or her to control the situation? Do I let my partner lead? What happens to me when my partner is in a position of power and control? Each of the proposed interventions offers another variant, as described below.

Intervention 1: The Leader and the Follower

Materials

Two A3 sheets of paper and a set of oil pastels.

Arrangement of the Therapy Room

The parent and the child sit at a table next to one another. A piece of A3 paper and set of oil pastels are laid out in front of them.

Instructions

In this exercise, one member of the dyad draws on the page with his or her eyes closed, while getting drawing instructions from the partner. The exercise is conducted in turns. Before the exercise begins, it is decided which member of the dyad will close his or her eyes first. The role of the partner whose eyes are open is to guide the other partner by giving instructions on how to draw on the page in a way that is relevant and fitting for the dyad. The partners can choose to lead however they feel most comfortable, by verbal instruction or by touch. After a few minutes of work, the partners switch roles and draw on a new sheet of paper. Both partners can decide on the number of colors to use and when to change colors during the exercise. A "warm-up exercise" can be done beforehand where one partner leads the other across the room with his or her eyes closed and they share their feelings regarding the experience.

Example

Rachel, 45, a teacher and mother of five, drew with Naomi, her 12-year-old daughter. Naomi is her youngest. Rachel chose to lead the first drawing (see Figure 9.1). She used touch, by wrapping her arm around her daughter's hand, and giving verbal instructions. At some stage during the work, Rachel asked Naomi if she would be willing to draw things from their trip together over the weekend and Naomi happily agreed. During the work process, Naomi cooperated and responded to her mother's instructions. She often asked questions to clarify details and requested more accurate guidelines. Toward the end of the exercise, Rachel suggested that Naomi draw the statues that they had seen on their trip. Throughout the exercise, Rachel encouraged her daughter with statements such as "Well done," and often drew on the page as well. At the end, Naomi stated that she did not always feel that she had the freedom to move around the page as she wished, but she trusted that her mother would lead her to draw beautifully. Occasionally, she felt that her mother was including her, but she sometimes felt "like her pencil." Rachel reported that she was trying to find a subject that would please her daughter and felt that she did a good job at leading the exercise.

In the second drawing (see Figure 9.2), when it was Naomi's turn to lead, Rachel suggested that they draw a field of beans that they had seen together. Naomi said to her: "Wait mom, first feel where the top of the page is so that you don't go outside of the lines." Naomi then guided her mother's hand along the edges of the page. Naomi accepted her mother's suggestion, but when Naomi assumed her role as the leader, Rachel made further suggestions for images for the drawing, selected the colors, and also drew without waiting for Naomi's instructions. When she needed help to position herself on the page, Rachel was not shy about asking for help. While they were working, Naomi expressed admiration for her mother: "Wow mom, you're drawing beautifully." Naomi encouraged her mother's independence and allowed her to initiate certain features of the drawing by asking her questions, such as "Do you want to draw the . . . ?" Rachel occasionally turned down her suggestions. Similar to the previous drawing, both partners expressed satisfaction about their work and commented that they were pleased with the result. However, both of them felt that Rachel had been the one to determine what content would be in the drawings, even when Naomi was the leader. They both agreed that the final product was essentially the work of Rachel.

Figure 9.1 Rachel, the mother, leads her daughter, Naomi

Figure 9.2 Naomi, the daughter, leads her mother, Rachel

Comments about the Exercise

As seen in the example above, distinctive leadership patterns can evolve during collaborative work. Observation shows that each specific dyad finds ways to deal with the task. In the exchanges that take place during the observation process, the participants talk about their feelings during the exercise: did the partner who was being led close his or her eyes throughout the whole exercise? How did he or she feel during the experience? What was he or she thinking about while being led by the partner? How does he or she feel about the end product and did it surprise him or her? Does he or she feel that the end product is the result of the partner's work or his or her own work? How does he or she feel? Did he or she make a drawing that met his or her expectations? How does it feel to see the end product? The patterns of behavior during the creative process are likely to reflect typical communication between the dyad. The therapist can help the participants explore whether these patterns are familiar, what they convey, whether they are appropriate for the continued relationship, and which particular behavior(s) should be changed.

In the case of Naomi and Rachel, it is important to consider the significance of Rachel's dominance in both her roles during the exercise and her tendency to adopt this role in both situations. Questions that can be discussed in this example include: does the mother find it hard to let others lead or initiate? Is it difficult for her to allow her daughter to be independent and assume control, or alternatively does the mother feel the need to strengthen her position as a leader in the family?

Intervention 2: The Chase

Materials

A half sheet of A1 cardboard, a set of markers, and a set of oil pastels.

Arrangement of the Therapy Room

The parent and child sit at a table next to one another. The materials are laid out in front of them on the table.

Instructions

In the first stage of this exercise, each member of the dyad selects one colored marker (a different color for each partner). One of the partners starts drawing a line on the page, while the other follows this line with his or her own marker. After a few minutes, the partners switch roles. During the creative process, the rhythm can be changed from fast to slow, or evading one another, and so on, similar to a game of tag. In the second stage, the partners observe how the process of chasing one another was documented on the page. They attempt to highlight any images they can see within the scribbled drawing and use oil pastels to add details to specific shapes on the page that further distinguish their shape. In the third stage, the partners write a story together about the different images that they identified together in their joint drawing.

Example

Dorine, a stylist and a married mother of three, drew with her middle son Ron who is in second grade. Ron chose a yellow marker and began to draw without talking (see Figure 9.3). Dorine followed the yellow line and drew with a pink marker. During the creative process, Ron occasionally paused and waited for his mother. He would look at her work, and sometimes comment that she had missed a section, or tell her: "You didn't do that correctly." In one instance, Dorine replied: "You are a perfectionist, Ron." Ron often tried to draw in distant parts of the page, or drew over certain lines that were already marked on the page. There was physical contact between the partners during the exercise.

In the next stage of the exercise and on the same page, Dorine chose a blue marker, and Ron chose a light green marker. They began to draw together and Dorine reminded Ron that it was her turn to go first. She drew a smiley face on the page, and in response Ron and the interviewer both commented that she should move around the page so that he could "chase" after her. Dorine laughed when she realized that Ron had understood the instructions better than she had, and then resumed drawing on the page. Much like Ron in his position as the leader, Dorine occasionally paused to allow Ron to catch up with her. Ron followed his mother's line,

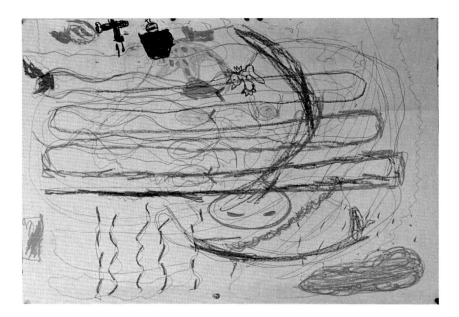

Figure 9.3 Ron and Dorine in the chasing exercise

but added extra details to his own lines. For example, when Dorine drew a straight line, he followed her with a wavy line.

When Dorine and Ron began identifying images in their drawing, different associations simultaneously arose as they talked. Ron mentioned that he saw the sea, and Dorine mentioned that she saw rain. In another image, Ron identified branches hanging down from a tree, a maze, and a lemon because it was a yellow oval, while Dorine identified a bush and an alligator. Another time Ron saw a wolf. When they began emphasizing the images they had seen, numerous other unconnected images were identified in the drawing. While she was drawing, Dorine also fiddled with her mobile phone, tried to communicate with the interviewer, and spoke with her oldest son who was also present in the room. She was distracted during the session and not fully devoted to the task. Perhaps in response to her behavior, Ron stopped answering her questions and instead focused on the drawing. He insisted on working on his own during the final stage of the exercise, and did not want to share his story with his mother.

In the interview that took place after the drawing task, Ron stated that he enjoyed the drawing exercise, but the story section was "just ordinary." Dorine mentioned that she enjoyed simply being together, and she was pleased to see her son's abilities. Dorine noted that she particularly enjoyed it when they complimented each other.

Comments about the Exercise

In this intervention, both partners created an unplanned dynamic and an evolving scribble while exchanging leadership roles. Various patterns of leadership behavior were reflected and emerged in the exercise, as well as the need for control, the merging of the partners, and their ability to be intimate together. The intervention process enabled both partners to express their inner worlds. This exercise expands the element of play and provides additional space for the expression of closeness or distance within the relationship. The joint drawing requires each partner to be attentive to the other. Through observation, each partner learns what images the other identifies within the drawing, whether they are willing to share them with one another, and how they will select the images they want to keep in the final work. In the third stage, the story element enters into the relationship. During the writing task, the images are assembled into one contextual framework. During this stage, it becomes clearer who is leading the work, the extent of the partnership within the dyadic relationship, and how the division of labor is carried out.

Ron and Dorine's drawing illustrates the disparity between the two partners in their commitment to the drawing task. Ron invested considerably in the process and it was important to him to follow instructions. His mother, however, was less focused on the task and let other issues interfere with their special time together. Perhaps due to this behavior, the remaining images were unrelated and Ron felt that the story was "just ordinary." This example demonstrates the potential of this exercise to create a ludic experience between members of the dyad.

Intervention 3: An Exercise in Nine Squares

Materials

A sheet or half a sheet of A1 cardboard, and one color of gouache paint selected by each member of the dyad (plus paintbrushes, jars of water, and cloths).

Arrangement of the Therapy Room

The parent and child stand together facing a board. A sheet of cardboard is tacked to the board. Each member of the dyad has his or her own art materials. By using a pencil or by folding the cardboard, the sheet is divided into nine equally sized squares (3 × 3).

Instructions

This exercise is carried out nonverbally. The parent starts by drawing a "question" (image) in color inside one of the squares (the upper right square). The child then "responds" with his or her own color in the same square without speaking. The purpose is to create an art-based dialogue that can be abstract in nature rather than portray concrete questions and answers. In the next stage, the partners exchange roles and the child "asks a question" in the adjacent square, and the parent "replies." They continue to progress between the squares in a similar fashion. Unlike the two previous interventions, the role of the "leader" in this technique is implemented for shorter and more specific periods and space on the page.

Example

Karen, a married woman with three children, drew with her middle son Jonathan, who is in first grade. At the beginning of the session, Karen sat on a chair and Jonathan sat on her lap. He either climbed or jumped on her, or fiddled with her hair, but Karen did not reprimand him for his behavior. She asked Jonathan to select a paintbrush, and offered to help him dip his paintbrush in the paint. He selected yellow for the exercise and Karen chose pink (see Plate 1). While working in turns on the page, Jonathan held his mother's shirt, and whispered to her, but she had a hard time hearing what he said. He found it difficult to follow the exercise and determine whose turn it was to lead, and Karen had to remind him many times. While working, Jonathan glanced at his mother to get permission to continue. Despite the concrete nature of the initial image and the anticipation of how to continue the image, the additional drawing and details made by the partner were original, surprising, and enjoyable. For example, when Karen drew a flower, she expected Johnathan to draw a stalk, but instead he added seeds, which surprised and delighted her. Most of the additions to the original drawings had an element of playfulness that was both unanticipated and fun. Inside one of the squares, Jonathan drew a picture of a sad girl, and Karen made some additions to the drawing to make her appear happy: "I saw a sad child and I don't like to see sad children, so I turned her into a happy girl with curly hair and she appeared full of life." Jonathan replied to his mom: "The drawing has no life! This girl is sad because I had nothing else to draw. To be sad is cool."

In another square, Jonathan found it difficult to draw the features of a face on a picture of a sun that his mother had drawn. He decided to turn the sun into a picture of a fox. When asked about the connection between the drawings they created on the whole page, Karen said that she thought that all of the images represented happiness, whereas Jonathan said it was all nonsense. Once again, he expressed disappointment that the picture of the sad girl was changed and turned into a happy one. Both Karen and Jonathan mentioned that they often felt misunderstood by one another, and that there was a decline in the level of mutual understanding during the work. Jonathan commented: "When my drawing changed [from sad to happy], she stopped understanding me, and this ruined my drawing."

Comments about the Exercise

When viewing the final work and examining one square after another, the experiences of the two creators becomes more apparent. As shown here, there is often an element of play involved in the exercise. Certain additions to the drawings were surprising, joyful, and even funny, but at times they could prompt a sense of frustration, a difficulty of being seen by others, or a sense of being misunderstood. During the exercise, the partners can contemplate various issues: did they understand each other? Did the communication flow smoothly or was it strained? What helped them understand each other? How did they feel at various stages of the process? Was there progress in the level of understanding as they moved between the squares? One useful technique is to ask the partners to try to make connections between the drawing experience and their real-life experiences living together at home. This exercise can be used to help parents and children stay longer in a nonverbal space where color and shape guide the process. Within this space, they both need to be attuned to one another to understand the implications of each other's drawings and then react accordingly. For Jonathan, who felt misunderstood during the exercise, the lack of words was a source of difficulty and led to further frustration.

Since both members of the dyad have equal status in this exercise (each member alternates with a question), there is neither a leader nor a follower. Rather, the partner's mutual intention leads into the next step of the process. A parent and child who can be attentive to one another will find themselves reacting agreeably in this exercise. In contrast, when problems arise in the way they are communicating, the therapist may stop the exercise and encourage them to talk about it during or at the end of the exercise.

10 Movement Exercises That Promote the Creation of Images

Introduction

Chapter 9 addressed leadership exercises in joint paintings. As part of these exercises, parent and child were encouraged to engage in active movement on the page, but often the final product remained abstract or unclear. This chapter presents three additional exercises that are also movement-oriented. However, in these exercises, the movement and play elements encourage the creation of concrete images that may represent the individual's inner world, and serve as a basis for observation. In all the exercises, the therapist invites the parent and child to participate in a joint game together that functions at different levels of regression. When the movement and play element of the exercise is over, they are asked to create an image from the end product.

Intervention 1: "Squiggle" (a Joint Scribble Inspired by Winnicott)

Materials

A4 pages and markers or colored pencils.

Arrangement of the Therapy Room

The parent and child sit at a table facing or next to each other. A stack of A4 sheets and colored pencils or markers are laid out in front of them. Each participant chooses one color.

Instructions

In this exercise, either the parent or the child starts drawing first and creates a single colored scribble on the page. The other partner is then handed the scribbled drawing and responds to the shapes he or she sees by attempting to draw a defined image from them with the marker or pencil.

This partner then gives the picture a title. Next, the partners switch roles and use a new sheet of paper. This exercise can be repeated as many times as the therapist sees fit.

Example

Erez, 42, drew together with his 6-year-old daughter Lital, who is in kindergarten. Lital chose to work with colored pencils and her father followed suit. Lital picked a silver pencil and her father selected a blue pencil. In this case, the parent and child played the squiggle game on the same sheet of paper (they did not use new sheets) so the entire process could be seen on one page (see Figure 10.1).

Stage A: Erez drew a wavy line and a vertical line in the center of the square. Lital added a horizontal wavy line and then stopped drawing. She claimed that it was an X.

Stage B: Lital drew a curvy swift line in the shape of the letter U. She looked at her father and said: "I'm curious to see what he will turn it into." Erez added details to the drawing and when Lital asked him what he was doing during the creative process, he answered: "What? You don't see it? It's a witch."

Stage C: Erez drew a wavy line. Lital moved her body and tilted her head toward her father and said that she did not know what to do. The interviewer told her she could make something up and that she could draw any made-up image. In response, Lital drew a line between the two ends of the wavy line to create a closed shape. Her father asked her about the shape she had drawn, and she responded by saying it was a heart.

Stage D: Lital drew a small arch on the page. Erez looked at the shape for a moment and then started drawing. He stated that he had drawn a teddy bear, and his daughter laughed and said that it was a teddy bear with a pig's nose.

Stage E: Erez drew a square and added a shape that looked like the number six. Lital said once again that she did not know how to continue, but a few seconds later she drew a closed shape. She started at the top of the line her father had drawn and added two lines, each with circular shapes. Erez said that it was a snail, and she agreed.

Stage F: Lital continued drawing freely and left a scribble for her father on the page. He started drawing and once again his daughter expressed curiosity about his drawing. She asked him what he was making. "Oh, it's a house!" She was excited when she understood his drawing. Erez confirmed her depiction and added that there was smoke coming out of the chimney.

Stage G: Erez drew a closed circle. Lital turned the circle into a figure, and when she finished she announced that she made a picture of a girl.

Stage H: Lital moved on to the next square and created a similar looking closed circle. She placed it at the bottom of the square and enlarged it. After

Figure 10.1 Erez and Lital create a joint squiggle drawing

a slight hesitation, Erez started to draw another circle inside the previous one. When Lital inquired about what he was drawing, he answered that it was a wheel and added a few diagonal lines next: "A wheel that sprays mud." When she heard his response, Lital repeated his words and smiled.

At the end of the process, the interviewer asked Lital and her father to invent a story that included some or all of the elements in their drawings. Lital answered that she couldn't find a relationship between the drawings and also couldn't invent a story. Her father smiled at her and said: "You don't see the story?" He continued and said: "Once there was a witch who lived in a house. One day she went to buy X's and sprayed mud on the girl. The girl got angry and cursed the witch. The witch was insulted and told the girl that she had no heart and said, 'So what if I'm a witch? I'm still good and I even helped a teddy bear, and since I helped him, he's been smiling.' When the witch returned home, a snail was waiting for her at the entrance." When Lital heard the story, she smiled and laughed.

Comments about the Exercise

The original squiggle exercise was developed by Winnicott as a way to create interactions and a playful space with his clients. In the version presented above, the therapist guides the parent and child through the exercise. If the exercise is meant for diagnostic purposes, a standard-size sheet of paper and only two colors should be used (so that each participant's work on the page is easy to see). If the main objective is therapeutic, multiple variations of the technique can be implemented. First, different materials and different size sheets can be used (e.g., A3 paper and oil pastels or cardboard and gouache paints). The exercise can also be done with many more colors (e.g., the original squiggle can be made with one color, but the image within the squiggle can be heightened or modified using a variety of colors). Finally, the stage following the drawing exercise can be expanded by asking the parent and child to write a story about the picture rather than simply telling one.

The assumption is that parent and child react to the initial abstract squiggle by projecting internal content. The output provides a window on the images that are characteristic of the parent and child and the content that is typical of their worlds. In the color selection stage, there may be a similarity between the colors and their dominance on the page as compared to the colors used by the partner. These choices may reflect facets of the representations of the relationship in many ways. For example, the choice of a strong and striking color for the self (e.g., black) and a light color for the partner (e.g., yellow) may reflect an inner reality in which the partner who is drawing may feel the need to stand out in order to protect him or herself in the relationship. During the squiggle drawing process, the level of complexity of the original squiggle may indicate the extent to which each participant wants to challenge the other. Some direct their partners by using a simple scribble that is easy to grasp (e.g., the first partner draws a circle with a few numbers on it to make sure that the partner will understand that it is a clock). Alternatively, parent or child may try their best to draw a complex squiggle that will challenge their partner and enjoy the surprise and creative elements that the partner will use in response. While the squiggle is being turned into an image, the level of creativity and consideration of the initial image can be observed. Some participants find it difficult to complete something that they did not start, whereas others will find the challenge very enjoyable. Mutual influences and relationships between the images can be observed during this stage, or whether each line added stands alone and functions autonomously. The way each partner watches and responds to the other during the creative process is also richly informative. This observation has great therapeutic value, which is inherent to focusing and accompanying the partner. After finishing the artwork, the partners can observe the sequence together. The therapist can ask the parent and child how they felt about creating an artwork using this technique. To what extent did the images surprise them or were they familiar? Did they find a connection between the different images? Naturally, they can be asked to explain what associations emerged in relation to the different images they drew.

In Erez and Lital's example, the parent and child were able to adapt to each other in a pleasant and playful atmosphere. The father started with a complex image of a "witch" (the profile of the image), which made

Lital, who does not possess the same graphic capabilities as her father, feel blocked and inhibited. After some persuasion from the interviewer, Lital continued working. At this stage, Erez realized that he had created a drawing at a standard that was too high for Lital and continued by drawing images that were simpler. Despite her initial difficulty, Lital began to understand the game with the two original simple images (an X and a heart), and later gradually created more complex images (a snail and a figure of a child). In the end, Erez helped Lital understand the story in a way that integrated the images on the page. In terms of color, Erez and Lital each selected different ones, but they each had a substantial presence on the page. In addition, they both created images that were similar in size. Due to Lital's age, it was difficult to talk to her about the interaction between her and her father. In this case, the story told by the father served as a form of closure for the entire exercise. If Lital had been slightly older, it would have been appropriate to ask her how she felt about the image of the witch her father drew in terms of its complexity, in relationship to her graphic abilities and the symbolic meaning inherent to the image.

Intervention 2: Animals in the Forest

Materials

Newspapers and a plastic sheet, thumbtacks, glue, oil pastels, A3 paper, white cardboard paper, water, brushes, rags and gouache paints, and bowls for water.

Arrangement of the Therapy Room

Two sheets of white cardboard paper are hung next to each other on the wall. The sheets are both hung at a height that the child can reach. The floor should be covered with newspaper and the wall behind the cardboard by a plastic sheet. Two color palettes should be prepared, one of which has cool colors (green, blue, and purple), and the other tones of brown. Jars of water should also be available.

Instructions

The participants spread water on the upper third of the cardboard sheet. Then, cold colors on the first palette are mixed to create more shades of green, blue, and purple. A considerable amount of water needs to be used to create blotches of color with a paintbrush (with light tapping movements). The colors trickle down and slowly cover the bottom part of the page. Next, the participants create shades of brown and fill in the gaps between the lines made by the cold colors of trickling paint. Together, this creates an image of a forest on the page. When the parent and child decide together that they have had enough of the painting stage, they both stop painting. At this point, the therapist asks each participant to imagine the following: "A calm and quiet place in nature. An animal is approaching [a real or imaginary animal]. It has its own color, its own special feel and special texture. Can this animal be touched? What does it feel like? How does it sound?" Each participant depicts an animal with oil pastels on an A4 page. They then cut out the picture and place the animal in the forest.

Example

Nechama, 35, drew together with Limor, her 6-year-old daughter. Limor chose to use a thick paintbrush and her mother used a thinner one (see Plate 2). The mother led the creative process: she took a bowl of water and placed it next to her, and repeated the instruction to only fill the "top third of the page." When the mother thought that they had both finished working on the upper third of the page, she concluded that the creative process was over (despite Limor's protest that she had not yet finished). They worked on both cardboard sheets and switched places.

Then, the interviewer demonstrated how to lightly tap on the page to create blotches of color, and Nechama and Limor started working together. Nechama noticed that Limor found it hard to create light taps of paint and suggested that she add more water to her paintbrush. Once more, Nechama reminded Limor that she should only paint on the upper third of the page and let the paint drip down the page. Finally, Limor said: "That's it," and the mother added: "You're tired."

While making the different shades of brown, the mother and daughter mixed the colors together for a long time. Afterwards, Nechama started filling the gaps between the lines on her side without looking or speaking to Limor. Nechama did not realize that Limor was struggling with the task and did not notice what was happening or try to help her daughter until the interviewer intervened. She suggested that Limor change paintbrushes and her position on the page. When Limor made an effort to create more shades of brown, her mother resisted. Nechama worked according to the instructions, whereas Limor made horizontal rather than vertical lines. This time, her mother encouraged her and assured her that she was being creative. She then asked out loud why she had not thought of doing that before. She then asked her daughter to "lend" her some of her creativity, if she wanted to.

During the animal drawing stage, Limor sat on Nechama's lap, and her mother caressed her and played with her hair. Afterwards, Nechama took a brown color and painted the head of a large figure in the middle of the page. Limor responded and said: "You drew a bear." Her mother replied in amazement: "How did you know?!" Nechama then draw a circle-shaped mouth and Limor said: "But I didn't want a scary bear." Nechama commented that it was a baby bear and it had a pacifier in its mouth.

Limor started drawing an image that resembled her mother's image, but hers was smaller. Nechama mentioned that she decided that the image was actually not a bear: "It's an imaginary animal, it looks like a bear, but also has wings and it's able to fly and also knows how to dive, so I'll add fins." Nechama tried to decide which animal Limor was drawing and she told her that it looked like a duck. Limor did not like her image and commented that she was unable to draw well. Nechama tried to reassure and encourage her. She also said she would swap drawings with Limor. The mother refused Limor's request to make a new drawing or to cut out the image for Limor. She simply suggested that Limor should "take her time." As a result, Limor continued to cut the page and Nechama encouraged her by saying: "Beautiful Papi, beautiful!! Who taught you to cut like that?" Limor replied: "You did." Toward the end of the exercise, the mother added fur to Limor's image, and it was no longer clear which image belonged to Limor and which image to Nechama.

Comments about the Exercise

The trickling paint stage enables a sense of release, liberation, and freedom, and often the unexpected use of many colors. It allows the participants to enjoy themselves and to explore an outlet of playfulness. This stage can be particularly important for families where issues of control, in any form, may arise. Nechama and Limor did not fully follow the instructions when trickling paint on the page such that mother and daughter did not take advantage of the opportunity to play with the water, get things wet, or drip on the surface. As a result, the marks that they created with the cold colors appeared composed and relatively dry. By contrast, when filling in the gaps between the lines they indeed complied with the instructions, which yielded a sense of organization such that this work appeared enclosed within a structured and calculated space. During this stage, Limor struggled to understand the instructions, which on the one hand led to difficulties, but later on to a creative variation based on the instructions.

These two stages, namely the trickling paint stage juxtaposed with the coloring of the trunks (gaps), offers a reversal of the two modes of functioning, which is their strength on an experiential level. This type of work is difficult for some people (it requires skill, control, and organization), and may lead to frustration. The theme of the forest and animals may be threatening, impulsive, or scary for some participants. This issue needs to be addressed and considered by therapists. The animal represents segments of the creator's inner world. It may express a desire (drawing a free bird or a powerful animal), it may also help to deal with anxiety (drawing a cute lion or a soft teddy bear), and it can also express drives. When the animal is placed in the shared forest, the discussion can center on what happens to the animal there. How does it feel in the forest? What happens to the part of the self that is represented as the animal in the forest?

In the Nechama and Limor example, as in other joint works, the creative work evoked themes of independence, dependence, and closeness in the relationship between parent and child. The transition between movement-based and sensory-based work to create a figurative image promotes different levels of functioning and may be challenging for some children. Limor, who struggled to take part in the first stages of the exercise, found it difficult to function independently when asked to create an image. This shows the transitions between the different stages of work and how this child coped with the different tasks during the session. Her mother often upheld and maintained the situation and occasionally allowed Limor to act independently. Throughout the entire joint work process, she tried to find ways to support Limor. The images that the mother and daughter chose to draw are informative as to the internal world of representations that emerged during the joint interaction session. Nechama's baby bear may represent issues of dependency. This bear compensates for its small size with its fantastic ability to fly, swim, and achieve anything it wants. By contrast, Limor's bear was a smaller version of her mother's bear. In the therapeutic setting, treating these images and understanding their significance for mother and daughter would constitute a crucial part of the self-discovery process.

Intervention 3: Splashing Paint with Syringes

Materials

Six syringes, gouache paints, 7–12 empty glass jars, stirring utensils (spoons, sticks), a bucket of water, two pairs of scissors, pins, white cardboard paper that is pinned to a wall, and plastic sheets/newspapers covering the floor sufficiently to make sure that the participants do not feel that they are making a mess in the room. There are also disposable aprons, white A3 and A4 sheets of paper, two sets of paintbrushes, and two palettes of gouache paint.

Arrangement of the Therapy Room

The white cardboard paper is pinned securely to the wall so it will not fall. The tables are positioned near the wall, 8–10 feet away, where the syringes and paints are placed. The floor and any valuable objects (such as books or curtains) are covered and protected with plastic sheets/newspaper. On a table in another part of the room, A3 sheets of paper are set out for each participant alongside paintbrushes, water, and a gouache palette to be used after the splashing stage. The participants prepare gouache paints by diluting them in water in a glass jar. Each jar preferably contains a different color, and the participants can be creative and blend new shades of color.

Instructions

Each participant cuts a shape out of a white A4 sheet of paper which constitutes "My shape." The participants pin their shapes to the wall with a few pins or attach tape to the back of the shape and stick it to the wall. Then, the parent and child take turns squirting colors. First the child and then the parent each fill a syringe with water and squirt the contents onto the wall, in turn. The order in which the parent and child squirt the paint should be maintained, and the therapist makes sure the order stays the same. Children may need help filling their syringes. During the second round, the parent and child each fill their syringes with one of the diluted colors on the table and try to squirt the color on the shape they made. There should be a few rounds of squirting paint and the participants can fill the syringe themselves with any color that they want. Each participant must have a turn in the same order. In addition, the participants can make a noise, a gesture, or say something while squirting paint.

Then, the parent and child remove their shapes from the wall, which at this stage are drenched in paint, and carefully place them on an A3 sheet of paper (the shapes are soaked in paint, and therefore it is better to move them together). Thereafter, each participant sits quietly in a separate corner of the room to add to the artwork with gouache paints and paintbrushes in the space on the page that surrounds the shape.

Example

Yael, a woman in her forties, a widow, and mother of two, drew with her youngest daughter Nofar, aged 11 (see Figures 10.2–10.5 and Plate 3). The interviewer asked them to sit at a table and cut a shape out of a sheet of paper. Nofar asked her mother to refrain from copying her, and her mother assured her that she would not. The mother commented that the shape that she cut for herself was ugly because it was crooked. Nofar finished cutting her image first and she commented that she did it perfectly. She then asked her mother to hurry up cutting her shape. When both of the cut images were complete, they pinned their shapes onto the splashing wall. The mother taped her shape on the wall at her height, while her daughter pasted hers at her own height. Thus, the shapes were placed at different heights on the wall.

Yael squirted her colors first and tried to create a "smiley" shape on the wall, but when the shape did not come out right she laughed with disappointment. Nofar chose to use purple and squirt color onto the wall. She discovered that the color can land on the surface in an unintended manner and said that it was fun, pleasant, and colorful, no matter what she did on the page. A ping-pong game of squirting paint on the wall began, with most of the paint landing on Nofar's shape. Yael did not notice that her

Figures 10.2–10.5 Yael and Nofar splashing paint with syringes together

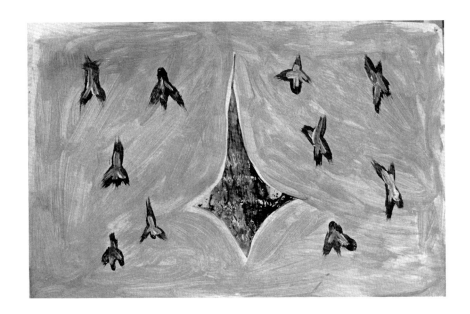

Figures 10.2–10.5 (continued)

shape had not yet been colored until after six rounds of squirting, and from that moment on, she oriented her squirts toward her own shape at the top of the page to add color. Nofar continued to focus on her own shape. When she saw how excited Nofar was, Yael gave her a few of her turns. Toward the end of this stage, Nofar looked at her mother's shape and squirted a purple "frame" around it, and in response her mother squirted a white frame around Nofar's shape.

Then, Yael and Nofar each removed their individual shapes from the wall. Nofar was annoyed when her shape tore accidently and she decided to complete the shape using her paintbrush. In the meantime, Yael started painting a blue background around her shape and filled the entire page. Nofar created rounded shapes with pink and purple lines in the background, and she repeatedly told her mother not to copy her work. Yael replied that she was not copying anything that she did on the page. Nofar continued painting and created blue shapes on the page, and then added colorful dots in different shades. As a finishing touch, she made a thick blue frame around the page and a red frame with different colored dots around her shape. Throughout the creative process, Nofar was worried that she would ruin her own work, but each time Yael assured her that she could not destroy it; with this reassurance, Nofar continued to experiment freely and playfully with the colors. Yael finished her background, which partly touched her star-shaped image. She added more stars to her shape so that the original shape was duplicated five times on each side of the original cutout shape, which were painted in dark blue with a white center. Yael finished before Nofar, and while waiting for her daughter she looked at her own work, as well as at Nofar's. In the end, the partners finished their paintings and complimented each other.

Comments about the Exercise

This exercise requires a great deal of preparation and organization, and a large enough room for the creative work, but the effort often constitutes a liberating experience through the use of color. The squirting stage symbolically represents content related to anger, destruction, leaving behind a mark, sexuality, and other themes. Accordingly, the associations that surface include concepts such as "shooting," "vomiting," or "elimination." The joint page and the shapes absorb the colors that contain content, reflecting each partner's internal drives from their private worlds and from their joint world, and thus containing them. The containing environment has to do with the capacity of the page to withstand and support the load and weight of the color, and its ability to reflect the content esthetically and in a way that it can be absorbed and processed. In the second stage, when each participant removes the shapes from the wall to start the individual work, there is a calming effect that complements the containment work: the large page with the squirted colors "contains" the emotional content and the colors that were squirted all over it, whereas in this stage the content returns, and is "placed" by the creator in a restricted manner for further processing.

The Yael and Nofar example shows how from time to time, an exercise that may seem liberating and playful can also evoke complex content related to dissatisfaction and fears about the quality of the artwork and its (in)appropriateness. Throughout the entire exercise, Yael was not satisfied with her artwork, which she thought was "crooked" and later seemed to lack color. In the final part of the work, Nofar also raised concerns that her image would be ruined and would not meet others' expectations. However, the process and the product included elements of play, freedom, and great pleasure. On the one hand, the transition from a creative free work to a more defined image leads to more possibilities within the work, and allows for relaxation and creating inner balance. However, this may also convey more complex content, such as the difficulty to accept the (unconscious) power of squirting, as well as dealing with a torn page and unwanted drops of paint. Yael and Nofar could have been asked after the exercise how they felt about the final product. Which sections were they satisfied with and which sections less so? They could also have been asked how they coped with similar situations in their lives when they were not pleased with their behavior.

11 Together and Alone

Introduction

This chapter presents eight structured techniques for creating joint drawings, all of which are characterized by their transitions between working in a private space and working in a joint space. They include a range of exercises that focus on the two central axes of the relationship: the ability to be alone and function autonomously, and the ability to be together and maintain closeness and intimacy. The opportunity to move between these spaces emphasizes their dual importance and the value in finding a balance between them, particularly in situations where one facet is prioritized at the expense of the other. Therefore, if there is dependency in the parent-child relationship, the partners are encouraged to create their own artworks in the presence of the other. Alternatively, if a parent and child are detached and have trouble connecting, they are encouraged to work in a structured manner toward joint activities that promote closeness and dependency. Each of these interventions constitutes a slightly different variant on these exercises, which the therapist selects as best suited to the parent and child's relationship, personalities, and needs.

Intervention 1: Colored Shapes on a Black Background

Materials

Sheets of colored paper in different shades, glue and Scotch tape, pins, paintbrushes, dampened pieces of chalk in different shades (it is also possible to work with oil pastels if the participants hesitate about working with wet chalk), and black cardboard.

Arrangement of the Therapy Room

Approximately one hour before the start of the exercise, the pieces of chalk are immersed in a bowl of water. The sheet of black cardboard is placed on the table, and the colored papers are laid out so that each one is visible. The parent and child sit at the table.

Instructions

First, each participant chooses one sheet of colored paper. By tearing (not cutting) the paper, they create a series of shapes that resemble each other but are different in size. The shapes can be uniform, amorphous, geometric, descriptive, and so on. Each participant takes the shapes and uses them to make a puzzle (by placing them on the table but not pasting them together). When they are finished, the parent and child observe their works together. Each takes a piece of the puzzle and pins it to their clothes. The remaining parts of the puzzle are collected and set aside. Then, each participant places three torn shapes on the piece of black cardboard. They can observe and rework the composition until they are both satisfied. They then glue the three shapes to the black cardboard. Next, the parent and child add more shapes to the black cardboard. After observing and agreeing on the position of the shapes, the remaining pieces are glued, excluding the shape that was pinned on their clothes and one other separate piece. Once the rest of the pieces have been glued to the page, both the parent and child find a location for the last shape and they explain why they chose that particular place on the page.

In the second stage, each participant chooses a piece of colored chalk that he or she likes and draws a line from one of his or her shapes on the black sheet toward another shape, and connects them. If there is another shape along its path, it must be avoided and gone around (it should not be drawn on). In addition, each participant can draw rays from their shape in any direction on the cardboard (e.g., toward the corners of the page), but avoiding the other shapes. By drawing rays/lines, different sections or a network of shapes are created on the black sheet of cardboard.

Then, each participant chooses a number of areas on the page, and colors them. During this process, the therapist can stop the exercise and ask the parent or child to decide together how they would like to fill the remaining empty spaces (with lines, dots, or by coloring in the entire space, or in any other way).

Example

Yoav, aged 45, the father of three children, drew with his oldest son, Yarden. Yoav described Yarden, his 10-and-a-half-year-old, as a sensitive child. Yarden chose to use blue paper and the father chose orange paper and asked if he could draw the shapes before tearing them. The father folded the page in half and carefully began to tear the shape of a circle. His son copied him and again inquired about the instructions and the size of the required shapes. After tearing a tiny shape, he said: "I made it really, really small, now I will create the biggest shape, I will fold the paper like this . . ." The father made two bowls from the circle, and Yarden arranged his torn shapes according to size and said: "The shapes are not exactly the same." When he noticed the bowls his father made, he asked: "Dad, how did you make two bowls from the same page?" Then he suddenly realized that he had another half of a page that he had not used: "Ah, I have another sheet, maybe I can make some more?" But then he decided that one was enough. When his father asked him: "Do you know what I made?" his son replied: "Bowls, right?" His father nodded and made another bowl that was bigger than the other ones. When they started working on the joint page, the father placed his bowls in the center of the page so that they formed a triangular shape. Yarden placed two of his shapes in the corners of the page and a third one between his father's two bigger shapes. Once they were satisfied with their composition, the interviewer asked them to look at their shapes and glue them to the sheet of cardboard. The son said: "I deliberately glued my shapes far from one another so that they would be separate and every shape would stand out on its own and would not be part of a series." When asked how a shape would feel if it were part of a series, he answered: "You can still see it, but it is only part of something." His father commented that he glued his shapes while thinking about the table setting: "Like a dinnerware set." When he was asked to glue another shape on the page, Yoav placed his shape further away, while Yarden placed his shape between the two big bowls that his father had made. When his father noticed this, he moved his shape closer to make another triangle that encompassed Yarden's shape. At this point, Yarden said: "When I saw that Dad made a circle, I wanted it to have a center. Like a tower surrounded by many small houses. For example, like a child who stands alone in the middle of a circle surrounded by people's arms, like when putting your arms around a tree." His father said that he initially placed the small bowl on the side: "I felt it was small and out of place. But then I was afraid it wouldn't look good and it wouldn't be good on the side, so I moved it toward the other ones." Yarden added: "Yes, it should be with all the other ones." The father replied: "When Yarden added his shape, the image suddenly appeared different to me. I felt the need to come toward him and in the direction he was going." When asked to choose a piece of chalk, Yoav chose white and Yarden looked for "a color that stands out." At first, they took turns drawing, but they quickly started drawing at the same time, and there was a feeling of harmony and mutual respect. Their lines seemed to connect the colorful shapes (see Figures 11.1–11.2 and Plate 4). When Yarden announced that he had finished, he asked his father about the little blue shape that did not have a connecting line, and then connected it himself. Yarden said they had made an ocean, and his father said it looked like the contour lines of a mountain on a map, and explained to his son about the markings of altitudes on maps. While drawing between the lines on the page, both father and son created images rather than using colors to fill in the gaps. The son drew a river, whereas the father drew repetitive geometric shapes of bowls. After consulting with Yarden on how to proceed, his son suggested adding handles or other colors. Yarden asked his father

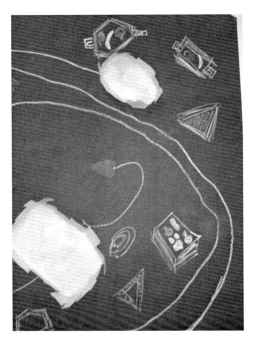

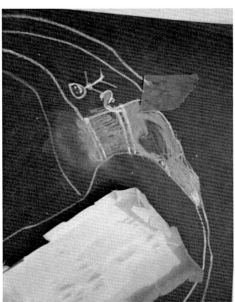

Figures 11.1–11.2 Yoav and Yarden create colored shapes on a black background

to add a boat to his river, and they both worked on the river and its vicinity. While they were working, the father asked about how to connect the images, and his son replied: "You can link them however you like. I connected the blue color of my shapes to the water of the river. For instance, here, the boat flipped over because the river is rough." While admiring the turbulent river, Yarden smeared the colors with his finger and said: "I wanted to draw a storm and the water that sprays when the waves splash, like when we were in Tel Aviv, eating ice cream, I remember that." When he finished, his father asked him to draw fruit together in the bowls. When they had finished, they both mentioned that they had enjoyed the exercise. Yarden said that he enjoyed drawing with his father when they each contributed to the drawing as a whole. The father acknowledged the help from his son and added that they did household chores and worked in the garden together, but they had never drawn together, and it was an interesting activity.

Comments about the Exercise

This exercise shows how the process of gluing the shapes on the page serves as the starting point for the joint work between parent and child. During the gluing stage, the shapes can be connected or they can be placed at a distance from one another. Some people like to have other shapes alongside theirs, and others prefer a secluded space. Thus, during the gluing stage when the parent and child paste their final shapes, the structure that was created in the beginning can be altered. For example, participants who may not like being left alone may connect their shapes to others. The therapist helps the participants consider what happened to the shapes they glued on the page: were the shapes left in isolation? Did the other shapes join them? How do they feel with what happened to them? The participants are also encouraged to think about the ways they oriented their shapes, and their location on the page, and what they learned from what they did. After the exercise, the final product is typically colorful and esthetic, and constitutes a pleasant positive experience. The chalk drawing stage forces the partners to have a certain amount of shared intentions and stylistic compatibility, which may be more important if there is a disparity between the parent and child's drawing abilities.

This exercise is safe and non-disclosing, and is suitable for an initial therapy session. It can certainly be used without verbal dialogue or interpretation, and the observation of the interaction can be done in a relatively non-threatening way. This exercise allows for a process of self-learning with regard to what happens to each participant during the session in terms of "what happens to me when I am being approached or when I am alone." In the joint work, there is an element of familiarity and a sense of unity, but also the element of surprise created by the dry and wet pieces of chalk, and the white sections of the paper when tearing the colored sheets of paper.

The work on the page is simple and protected and does not require any prior knowledge. Hence, there is less pressure to do well on the activity, but there is a great deal of information about the relationship between parent and child that can be gleaned while observing the creative process.

In the example described above, the work became a metaphor when father and son placed the shapes on the page. Two primary wishes were apparently expressed. The first was the boy's desire for a separate and individual existence and not to be seen as "part of a series." At the same time, and perhaps in a more powerful manner, there was a craving for intimacy and a close connection between father and son. This was conveyed in the way the shapes were positioned on the page and the connecting lines between them, and also in Yarden's efforts to connect the final small shape to the others. Interestingly, despite the strong mutual desire for cooperation and a connection, during the latter stages of work, there was a great disparity between the images created by the father and the son. This disparity would have been interesting to discuss in a therapeutic context. Despite the father's wishes, the images did not connect and communicate with one another, but Yarden and his father were able to help each other work on them.

Intervention 2: Connect the Circles on the Cardboard

Materials

A half sheet of cardboard, two dinner plate size paper circles (cut or drawn on the shared cardboard page), oil pastels, gouache paints, plastic cups, paintbrushes, masking tape, and pencils.

Arrangement of the Therapy Room

The parent and child sit side by side or facing each other at the table. The two circles of paper are placed on top of the half sheet of cardboard (preferably held down with tape).

Instructions

First, the parent and child are each asked to draw their own circles using oil pastels. Then, they are asked to choose two gouache colors and mix them together in their plastic cups. Next, the participants draw further away from their own circles toward the circle of the other participant by creating a colored path on the page with the new gouache color they mixed in the cup. Each step toward the other circle can have a task associated with it. For example, the participants can be asked to mention something good or bad that happened that week, or talk about something they like or dislike, and so on. Once the page has been divided by the various journey lines, the parent and child are requested to fill in the gaps between the lines (until the page is full). This task can also be accompanied by music. In this setting, the parent and child walk or dance around the table while the music is playing, and each time the music stops they go to the table to work.

Example

Asaf, a 38-year-old father who has been divorced for five years, drew with his only child, his 7-and-a-half-year-old daughter, Tamar. Although the father was sick, they both attended the session because Tamar refused to give up the opportunity to draw with her father. At the beginning of the exercise, the father expressed apprehension when he saw the size of the page. Later, he repeatedly expressed his dissatisfaction with the exercise, and mentioned that it was too long. When asked to paint in their own circles (see Plate 5), the father asked: "What should I do inside?" and Tamar asked: "Can you also write?" The daughter wrote the word "Ballerina" inside her circle and began to paint, while her father watched her and was unable to start drawing. A few minutes later when he started working, Tamar paused for a moment and looked at him. After approximately 20 minutes, the daughter said that she had painted a ballerina on a stage. Later, she shared her positive experience as a dancer in her dancing class, where she had a major role and felt loved by her teacher. The father said that he painted the sea, seagulls, and a boat. The father and daughter placed their circles in the center of the page and glued them down. They only noticed that their drawings were glued in opposite directions at the end of the exercise.

Then, in the next stage, and in accordance with the instructions, the daughter poured yellow and red gouache into a plastic cup and mixed them together. Her father complained and said that those were the exact same colors that he wanted to use, and then selected blue and white instead. When asked to draw a path between the circles and mention something positive that happened to them during the week, the daughter talked about the fun she had at her Hanukkah party and her father told her about his successful project at work. When they were asked to talk about something they disliked, the father said: "I don't like it when Tamar is undisciplined and rude, and I don't like having unresolved issues at work." Tamar replied and said: "I don't like it when I make a mistake in my notebook and I need to fix it." During their conversation, the father and daughter continued to draw their paths, and it became evident that the father was imitating Tamar's paths and drawing his paths as a mirror image of hers. During the last stage of the exercise, the coloring stage, the father colored the spaces around his daughter's circle in pink and mustard, and then repeated the same thing around his circle. Tamar painted the bottom of the page in green and black, and added white above this area of the page. Eventually, the father became tired and said so to his daughter. His daughter tried to encourage him to continue and he tried to smear the colors the way she was doing. During the exercise and the discussion thereafter, it became clear that the daughter was enjoying the creative process, particularly the painting and her interactions with her father. She liked using the paint and enjoyed handling the material, and was not afraid of getting dirty. By contrast, it was clear that the father did not enjoy the painting process and made an extra effort to draw because his daughter asked him to. He told his daughter that he was happy to see she was enjoying herself during the exercise and that made him want to go on drawing himself. During the work process, the father was aware of his daughter's moves and was attentive to what she was saying. In the end, they both agreed that she was the leader during the creative process.

Comments about the Exercise

This exercise was characterized by an abundance of playfulness and a sense that something enjoyable was happening in the room. This exercise, like the previous one, is suitable for the initial stages of therapy due to its structured nature and non-threatening level of creativity. The participants can work on the exercise together as a moment of shared experience and enjoyment. From a diagnostic perspective, a great deal of information about the relationship between parent and child can be derived from the exercise without the need for dialogue or explicit requests for interpretation.

Although the father was tired and sick, he made the effort to take part in the exercise that was so important to his daughter. In this example, the participants placed their circles on the page, but in other circumstances the therapist can do so beforehand, or alternatively they can be drawn directly onto the sheet of cardboard. If the parent and child place the circles on the page themselves, this also conveys information about their relationship, and primarily about the need for closeness or the desire for separation. In this example, Tamar and Asaf's mutual desire to be close to each other was demonstrated by the positioning of their circles. When the participants have finished drawing inside the circles, they can be invited to discuss the final product and share their thoughts on the images. In terms of relationship, the circle represents the personal and private space that cannot be permeated. When there is the fear of entry into this personal space, the parent and child can draw a boundary around each circle and work within it. The personal circle serves as a space where each participant can express content from their private worlds. In this example, the daughter used her private circle to express dancing—an experience that she loves, a place where she is successful and feels appreciated. She revealed and expressed positive experiences to her father. It is possible that she was expressing her wish for a similar position in her relationship with the father.

During the joint creative work stage, there is reference to the relationship and work on the space within the relationship. Due to the structured nature of the exercise, every departure or variation on the guidelines can easily be seen: did the partners move away from their frames and did they get to their partner's frame? Did they enter it or not touch it at all? Did they choose a short path or a long and winding one? How were the gaps filled? Who used more space and who used less? Were there differences in their pace of work? What verbal responses were expressed during the activity? Was it a pleasant and playful experience, or was there a sense of rivalry? If appropriate, all of these issues can also be verbally clarified after the exercise.

Intervention 3: The Forest

Materials

Half a sheet of cardboard, several A4 sheets of paper, oil pastels, scissors, gouache paints, palettes, paintbrushes, jars of water, rags, and masking tape.

Arrangement of the Therapy Room

The parent and child sit side by side at the table. There are A4 sheets of paper and oil pastels on the table. In another part of the room, a sheet of cardboard is tacked to a board, and next to it there are gouache paints and the other drawing and painting implements.

Instructions

First, the parent and child are asked to draw a number of trees on their own separate pages. They are then asked to cut the trees out and then place their trees provisionally on the sheet of cardboard. They can change the position and adjust their trees as many times as they want until they are both satisfied with the final composition. Last, they are asked to paste their trees to their joint forest, and can add other trees, objects, or images that can be painted in the joint forest. These additional objects can be made with gouache paints.

Example

Yaakov, 43, drew with his 8-year-old daughter, Shachar. Each of them began by drawing their trees separately. Shachar drew two big trees that were later located on the right side of the joint drawing, and the father drew five smaller elongated trees that were later located in the center of the joint drawing (see Figure 11.3). As requested, they worked separately on the drawings and did not look at each other's work during this stage of the exercise. Despite knowing that they would need to cut out their trees from their individual pages, both Yaakov and Shachar added a background of earth and sky to their drawings. When they were finished, Shachar asked whether her drawing was pretty, and the father asked for the next instructions.

They then cut out their trees and the surrounding earth from the paper. They sat close together with their shoulders touching and collectively planned how to glue their separate trees onto the joint page. The process was a joint decision, and was accompanied by questions concerning each other's preferences. The daughter started pasting the trees onto the joint page slowly and meticulously while her father encouraged her calmly and softly, while holding segments that she had not yet glued. While she was applying glue to the trees, Shachar noticed that her tree was concealing part of her father's tree, and she said: "But the tree is on top of your tree." The father told her that it was all right and pretty, and she continued pasting the rest of the trees. Once the trees were glued to the page, they were asked to paint a forest in the background using gouache. The daughter asked how to make the color brown, and the interviewer explained this to her, whereas her father told her: "Go with the flow . . . It doesn't have to be exact." The father painted a tree that resembled his daughter's trees on the left side of the page and his daughter added some earth underneath. Afterwards, she painted two trees that resembled her father's original trees, and when she finished, she suggested that they add the sky and the sun to the drawing. The father agreed, and together they added more details to the joint work. Occasionally, their hands crossed over and they drew past each other's positions on the page. At the end of the process, they both admired the painting and its beauty, and commented that it was fun to work together. The exercise on the joint page allowed for a large amount

Figure 11.3 Yaakov and Shachar draw a forest together

of physical contact between them, and they seemed to enjoy this sense of closeness. They often smiled, helped, and listened to each other, and encouraged each other during the creative work.

Comments about the Exercise

Similar to the two previous exercises, this exercise focuses on individual images that integrate into a unified image that represents the relationship between parent and child. In this case, the subject was a forest, but it could easily be replaced by another subject of interest to both participants (e.g., a city with houses, a road with cars, a field of flowers, a zoo, etc.). During the first stage, which addresses the personal image, the image that each participant creates within the context of the relationship can be observed. As a function of the child's age, the participants can be asked to talk about the pictures they made. Younger children can be asked to tell a short story and older children can be asked what it represents to them. In the second and third stages, the relationship plays a central role and the therapist can stop briefly at any time to ask about the dynamics between the participants: where did they chose to position their images (near or far from one another, in the middle, or on the side of the page)? Were they satisfied where their partner positioned his or her images, and if not did they dare to reposition them? How was the joint work expressed and how were the different roles assigned to each participant? And finally, how did they feel during the process, how deeply did the process reflect the relationship between them, and what did they think about the final artwork?

In the Yaakov and Shachar example, it was clear that both the parent and child were trying to form ties on the page and bridge the differences that emerged in the original tree drawings. They worked harmoniously and cooperatively. Both participants made an effort to engage with the other's pictures as well as their own – the father drew a tree in a style that resembled Shachar's tree and she drew two trees that resembled her father's tree. However, there was no attempt to extend and develop the drawing, and in the end the drawing only contained trees, the earth and a skyline. When Shachar wanted to stop and contemplate (whether to place one tree on top of another) or expand the process (an attempt to create the color brown), her father simply responded that it would be better to "go with the flow" and spend less time on the creative process.

Intervention 4: A Joint Collage

Materials

Half a sheet of cardboard, colorful magazines (the therapist can also supply cutout and prepared pictures), glue, a pair of scissors for each participant, and oil pastels.

Arrangement of the Therapy Room

The parent and child sit side by side at the table. The half sheet of cardboard and other materials are placed on the table in front of them.

Instructions

The parent and the child are asked to select four images that they like from the magazine – these can be pictures that attract their attention or pictures that represent their personalities. The choice can be made individually or they can be on a specific theme as a function of the therapeutic objective (e.g., if a family is about to move, the participants can be asked to select images that represent the place they are leaving or the place they are going to). After the pictures have been selected and cut out from the page, each participant presents and briefly explains the pictures they selected.

Then, the parent and child are asked to paste the pictures onto the joint page. They need to decide together where to place each one and should discuss the composition of the page until they come to an agreement. Finally, they are asked to use the oil pastels to fill in the spaces between the pictures to create a whole, complete collage.

Example

Sharon, aged 37, was drawing with her 7-year-old son, Tom. The session took place after Tom finished school at a time when he would normally watch television at home. Initially, he opposed the idea and refused to cooperate, and insisted that he was only going to talk and not do anything else. His mother encouraged him to participate by compromising and promised to give him treats if he attended the session (candies and additional television hours). The mother chose two nature magazines from the collection, both for her son and for herself. She asked Tom how they should choose the images and gave him a number of alternatives. Together, they decided that each would select two images. Tom quickly selected two images as though he wanted to get the job over with. His mother chose one picture and started to cut it out from the page. Tom told her that he was not cutting anything out from the page. The interviewer suggested that he tear the images from the page and he tried tearing his images. His mother offered to cut the images out for him and asked him to look for another picture while she was busy working.

Sharon said that she chose a picture that reminded her of Harry Potter. Her son said that he had selected "cool" images: the first picture was a man who Tom thought looked like a sorcerer; in the second picture, there was a huge pair of chopsticks holding a plane in the sky—"It's funny and arbitrary"—and in the third image, there was a man in the countryside (but before gluing the third picture down, Tom swapped it for a picture on the other side of the page). While gluing Sharon once again asked for her son's opinion and went along with what he wanted. Tom put all the pictures together on the right side of the page, tightly packed on top of each other (see Figure 11.4). He then asked his mother to glue them down onto the page for him. When asked to draw and paint around the pictures, the mother asked Tom what he wanted to do. He did not respond, so she offered to paint a castle, like the one in Harry Potter, and he agreed. She began drawing the outline of the castle in a large empty white space on the page. Tom told her that she did not make Hogwarts very accurately, and she responded that he could draw it himself. In response, Tom said that he did not know how to draw on such a large scale. It appeared that he was not happy with her drawing and wanted to tease her. Tom then suggested that his mother add the picture of Harry Potter with a broomstick, but his mother insisted that if he wanted this in the drawing, he should draw it himself. Tom acquiesced and drew the broomstick and then added the figure of Harry Potter dressed in a robe and holding a wand in his hand. He called him fat Harry Potter (the robe made him look plump). He devoted a lot of effort to the drawing and emphasized every little detail and line. Meanwhile, the mother continued to fill in the empty spaces in the castle drawing and also added the sky. When Tom finished drawing Harry, he talked about another character from the book that the mother knew as well, and he said that he wanted to draw him. Again, he asked his mother to draw the character instead of him, but she said no. They talked about what the character should look like, and that

Figure 11.4 Sharon and Tom create a joint collage

he has a droopy face. Finally, the mother agreed to paint only the face, because she said she did not know how to draw the whole figure. While the mother was looking through the colors, the son began to draw the body, and in the end he drew the whole figure, even though he had said that he would only draw the body. He drew a tiny face relative to the large body. At this point, he was already immersed in the playful atmosphere and the experiences of the characters as they attacked each other. At first, the character shot red fire with its wand ("Which is the exact same color as Harry's wand," Tom said). The mother asked: "Red fire?" and the son answered: "Sure," and demonstrated with his voice how the fire sounds. He also stood up and mimicked the scene and he gave the impression that he was really enjoying the game. Every time he added another line, more fire and other details, he said: "I should add just one more little thing." When he was finished, and the interviewer announced that the exercise was over, he ran to the television, but returned a few moments later to add a meteor, and said that they are fighting each other. When asked how he felt about the end product, he said that he was satisfied.

Comments about the Exercise

As with the previous exercises, this exercise reflects the space of the relationship between parent and child. On a personal level, the participants are attracted to their individual preferences, and select the images that they want, and can choose how and to what extent they share their personal experiences with their partner. On a relationship level, the parent and child are required to work together. They need to choose where to position each of the images. This can be carried out in turns or simultaneously. These decisions are made as a function of the therapeutic objectives. In any case, the parent and child need to create an art product. The therapist can stop the exercise after the placement of the pictures to inquire how the process feels to them thus far, make sure their images were glued correctly, and ask what happened during the decision-making process (this discussion can also be held before the gluing stage, which lets the participants make changes in the composition). During the last stage of the exercise, the parent and child are asked to work together. They have to decide what happens in this space and how they will work within it (taking turns, dividing the page, assigning individual tasks, etc.). All of these decisions can be discussed at the end of the exercise.

In this exercise, the therapist can change the size of the sheet of paper. If the space is small and crowded, the parent and child have less space to work, and they will have to establish their places together on the busy page. Alternatively, if the paper is larger, the images can be further apart. These choices are informative of the search for proximity/distance and provide an opportunity for more extensive therapeutic work regarding the images.

   In Sharon and Tom's work, several impressive developments occurred during their session. Sharon surprised Tom when he got home from school and asked him to work creatively with her. This disrupted his schedule, and initially he did not like the idea and refused to participate. Later, it was obvious that he became absorbed in the world of imagination and creativity and enjoyed working with the images. Second, despite their decision to choose two images separately, the mother actually only chose one picture, and that seemed to be more connected to Tom's inner world rather than to hers. As the exercise unfolded, the drawing told Tom's story that drew on his very vivid imagination. When looking at the drawing, it was easy to recognize Tom, but difficult to learn about the inner world of his mother. Perhaps this dynamic, in which Tom is present, prominent, and leads the process, and where his mother makes space for him, may reflect their relationship. Alternatively, Sharon's work could have been influenced by her attempt to persuade Tom to join in, which would make the provision of space an explicit choice on her part. During the creative process, she encouraged her son to work independently, refusing his request to draw for him and encouraging him to draw for himself.

Intervention 5: Warm and Cool Colors

Materials

Two sheets of cardboard paper, each cut into a 30 × 30 cm square, a large sheet of paper, paintbrushes, rags, water, gouache paints, and glue.

Arrangement of the Therapy Room

Four color palettes are placed on the table, two of which have the cool colors along with white, and two with the warm colors along with white separately.

Instructions

The parent and child each select a palette of colors (cool or warm), and make an abstract, unrestricted painting on the square sheet of cardboard. They are asked to fill the entire space with color and paint in a free manner. Then, they take a palette from the second family of colors, and once again create an abstract painting on another square sheet of cardboard. Once each participant has finished painting the two square sheets of paper, they decide together whether they want to continue the exercise with cool or warm colors. Each participant individually considers where to place his or her square sheet of paper in relation to the other within the joint space. They can try out the positions of the sheets before gluing them down on the large sheet of paper. Finally, the parent and child decide together how to work in the joint space and how to fill in the empty space. The only precondition for this stage of the work is that the parent and child use the same palette that was used for the colored square sheets of paper.

Example

Efrat, 30, drew with her oldest daughter, Mor (the eldest of four children). Mor is 7 years old. At the beginning of the exercise (see Figures 11.5–11.6 and Plate 6), Mor was very hesitant as to which palette to choose, and while she was still deciding, her mother selected a palette with warm colors and Mor followed suit. While working on their individual drawing, each made marks on the page that at some point touched each other. There was a similarity in their drawings in that they painted their colorful marks and left the white spaces that connected them, which was most likely a result of their constant eye contact and observation of each other during the process. At the end of the first stage of work, the mother complimented her daughter on her drawing and said: "It's so beautiful," and Mor smiled happily. In the second individual drawing with the palette with cool colors, the mother once again began drawing first. Her daughter, who was watching her draw, tried to imitate the circular movements that she made in the center of the page, and then made diagonal lines at the bottom of her page. The mother also observed her daughter's drawing and used a similar pattern of colors. The mother encouraged Mor to join her in smearing where they both used their fingers to smear the colors on the page without a paintbrush. After approximately 10 minutes of work, they were both happy to hear that they would continue painting together on the joint page with gouache.

After a joint discussion, the mother and daughter placed the sheet of paper between them. Mor said that she liked the warm colors because she likes to draw the sun shining as well as the mountains. Her mother asked: "So, do you want to pick the colors that you're used to, or do you want to try something new?" The daughter chose her preferred warm colors. Mor placed her drawing in the corner of the page close to her side of the page. Her mother placed her square nearby, centered at the bottom of the page, with the drawing at the edge of the page. When given the opportunity to change their positions, the daughter turned her drawing so that it was also at an angle.

During the gluing stage, Mor turned her drawing over to apply glue to the page. The gouache paint that was still wet left a mark on the sheet. Mor was disappointed and decided to paste her drawing over it, to "hide the dirty mark she made." She had trouble gluing the corners of the page that had curved upwards when it was drying and her mother helped her. Her mother said: "What do you suggest we do? I think that maybe each of us should use the technique we used in our individual drawings and use it together on the bigger page." Mor replied: "Yes, we can do it like this with the paintbrush [she demonstrated] and you can also use your fingers [again demonstrated]."

Her mother asked: "And how will we connect our drawings?" Mor suggested they draw a big heart between their two drawings: "As if the drawings are friends." After talking, they went to work on the joint drawing. The mother drew the outline of a heart, and Mor filled it in. A few minutes later, Mor suggested they paint with their hands, and her mother liked the idea and expanded on it: "We can draw with our fingers, a butterfly, and even a centipede." The daughter became excited: "Yes, we can also draw a flower and a heart." The cooperation between the mother and daughter, the creativity of the artistic process, the brainstorming and mutual acceptance of ideas, as well as the mother's provision of help when it was needed, continued during the joint work. In the discussion after the creative work, the two of them shared their joyful experience of creating together. The daughter mentioned that she enjoyed deciding things together, and learning new things from her mother. Mor and her mother stated that they felt that there was space for all of their ideas during the joint work. In the end, Mor asked if she could hang the drawing in her room.

Comments about the Exercise

As with the previous exercises, there is room for both individual and joint space in this exercise. However, in this exercise, the playful element with the different families of colors encourages a sense of release, freedom, and playfulness. The artwork is created from an emotional space where there is no burden or pressure to succeed. In this example, there was reciprocity between mother and daughter from the start, when the daughter understood and imitated what her mother was drawing.

In the transition to the joint space of the drawing, parent and child each provide a completed drawing of equal size, which allows each of them to have a clear, defined place on the joint page. Although the mother is older and more knowledgeable, she and her daughter can cooperate and reach an agreement as to their equal contribution to the joint space. The opportunity to change the position of the personal drawings encourages the partners to consider and relate to each other. The shift from an individual drawing to a joint drawing compels the partners to engage in a discussion and a decision-making process. The repositioning of the individual drawings affects what happens to the parent and child, and requires a certain amount of courage and capacity to contain the other. The joint work requires both partners to adjust to each other, and each of them (depending on the age of the child) can assess their ability to contain their partner's world, with the different rhythm and the language that resides within them (in the drawing much like in everyday life). This allows them to discover what they have in common. During the joint process, there are often specific "words" from each individual's "drawing language" that become the language of both partners. In the example above, the action of smearing colors with their fingers that they both enjoyed in the individual drawings (initiated

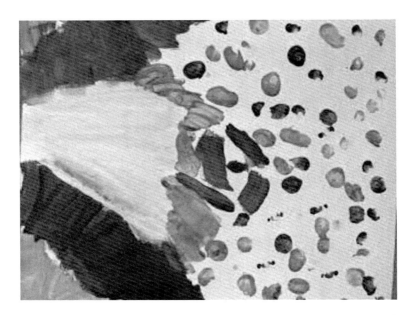

Figures 11.5–11.6 Efrat and Mor draw together using warm and cool colors

by the mother) became the primary method in the joint drawing. When the partners agree on this choice, as was the case for Efrat and Mor, this can create a sense of sharing, closeness, and support.

The therapist can raise a number of questions: what family of colors did they relate to better? How did they place the two shapes in relation to each other? Touching at the corners? Overlapping? Separated? How did each partner feel about the position of the individual drawing in the joint space? How did the joint discussion proceed? Were both of their voices heard? Did each consent to the changes? How did each partner relate to the other's drawing? What did each partner feel about the joint work? In the example, the mother and her daughter reported enjoying the joint creative process and happily agreed on how to proceed together.

Intervention 6: Working on Thirds of the Page

Materials

A sheet or half a sheet of white paper, one color of gouache paint for each participant (of their choice), paintbrushes, water jars, and rags.

Arrangement of the Therapy Room

The parent and child sit at the table and face each other. The sheet of paper is placed between them and they each have individual art materials. The sheet is divided into three sections: one faces the parent, one faces the child, and the third one is between them.

Instructions

The parent and child each make an abstract drawing in their own styles on the third of the page that is closest to them. Then, they draw together in the middle third. A variant on this exercise can be carried out without verbal communication.

Example

Ya'ara, aged 35, drew with her eldest son Shai, aged 10. Ya'ara is remarried and has two sons. The mother and son sat down to work (see Plate 7). She started to draw a sun, but when she was told that the drawing should be abstract, she painted across her sheet with three colors: turquoise, green, and brown. Shai selected a thick paintbrush and painted a light blue spot at the bottom of his section and then added waves above it in the same color. His mother painted green dots on a brown background by lightly tapping with the paintbrush, and then used the same technique to create red dots on a green background. She explained her drawing by saying: "Here are a few flowers." She then added purple spots randomly between the red dots. Shai asked if he could paint using his fingers, and he was pleased to be told that he could. He took a darker blue color with his finger, made a mark in the center of the turquoise mark, and explained: "I'm mixing the color slightly and creating all kinds of backgrounds, look how the dark blue is sinking into the turquoise color." He then commented that he needed a new color for his painting, and selected yellow. He wanted to mix two colors together and his mother encouraged him: "Mix them, don't be afraid." The mother added a little blue spot to the turquoise mark that she made at the top of her page, and announced that she was finished. Shai continued to work and mixed his colors, and he seemed pleased that he was the center of attention. He painted a yellow semicircle above the orange-brown mark on the page and filled the semicircle with color. He then chose a thicker paintbrush and painted rays for the sun by alternating between orange and yellow rays. He added a white face to the sun, looked at it, and smiled. His mother complimented him on the way he was working and said: "You are working so beautifully." He continued to work for roughly 15 minutes after his mother finished her section.

In the joint drawing, Ya'ara suggested that Shai should draw a house and said that she would add the surrounding sky and garden. Shai agreed and started painting a brown outline of the house, a door, and a handle. His mother asked what weather he would want to make for their painting. He thought about it and said: "Warm and pleasant, like today." The mother responded: "Then the sky is clear," and she painted turquoise clouds at the top of the page. She added green spots next to the house and a tree. She said that she would paint a lemon tree similar to the one they had in their garden and added yellow dots by lightly tapping her paintbrush on the page. She suggested Shai should add green leaves to her tree, and they then painted the leaves together. The son then painted an orange roof on the house. His mother asked him: "Who lives in this house?" He replied: "We will write 'Family . . .' We don't have to write who is living here, it's okay like this." The mother suggested writing anyway, and finally he wrote his last name. The mother responded: "Now we need your father to come and mop the floor to clean up what we did . . ." and they both laughed. In the discussion after the exercise, Ya'ara said she noticed that they both painted suns in their individual drawings, and therefore both wanted their suns to be present in their joint drawing. The son added that he thought that they both painted the surrounding area of the house and made the house together in the middle of the page.

Comments about the Exercise

Similar to other art-based interventions, this exercise enables a shared playful experience between parent and child. Unlike the previous exercises, in this exercise the parent and child are not asked to create a background for their individual spaces, but rather to take their own styles and content into the joint space. For example, in Ya'ara and Shai's drawing, Ya'ara believed that the joint drawing should contain a sun because they each painted suns in their own drawings. Shai, on the other hand, argued that since each of them drew a background in their own drawings, the link in their joint drawing should be made by drawing their house in the middle of the page. The playful element can be further developed by adding more colors to the drawing, providing a choice of other colors, different paintbrushes, and so on. When necessary, the boundaries between the spaces on the page can be delineated with a pencil, or by connecting spaces with different colors.

The individual space provided to the parent and child in this exercise demonstrates and highlights the private space that each partner lives in, as well as their shared interactive space. These two spaces are presented side by side: "I am alone, I am by your side," and "I am together with you." Each of these may provide an alternative or additional way to express imbalanced behavior. The partner's movement between these spaces of separation and cooperation provides a window on the relationship and how they handle the transition between worlds.

The different styles can be examined at the end of the creative process and how they came together on the last third of the page. Were the different styles maintained in this space? Did they integrate or did one dominate? Were there areas where the partners drew on top of each other or did their styles merge? What characterized the experience of working together? Similar to the other parent-child exercises, the therapist can ask both participants to think about the connections between their drawings and their relationship.

Intervention 7: From a Half to a Whole Drawing

Materials

A3 paper and oil pastels.

Arrangement of the Therapy Room

The parent and the child sit next to each other at the table. A sheet of A3 paper and oil pastels are placed on the table and the paper is folded in half.

Instructions

The child is asked to start drawing on half of the page up to the middle. It is important for the child to understand that the parent will continue the drawing, and therefore it should be a subject that can be resumed and continued. The parent observes the child during the creative process and tries to understand the child's method of drawing: the colors, intensity, style, lines, and so on. Subsequently, the parent is asked to complete the drawing while the child observes the parent.

Example

Leah, aged 54, drew with her son, Ron, aged 14 and a half. Ron started drawing (on the right side) by creating a green line to demarcate the ground (see Figure 11.7). Accidentally, he drew the line across the entire page. When his mother and the interviewer reminded him about the rules, he claimed that he had forgotten. Shortly after, the mother praised the quality of his drawing: "How beautifully you are drawing," and he thanked her with a smile. The mother then said: "What a beautiful smile you have. Don't draw outside of the lines, okay?" Ron drew a house, grass, and a tree, and applied a lot of pressure with his pastels.

When it was the mother's turn to draw, she started adding oranges to the tree that her son had drawn, despite his objections. When she began to draw on her assigned half of the page, she drew a house and asked whether the drawing should be similar to her son's drawing. She then looked at her son and at the interviewer, and said that she wanted to draw a man but did not know how to draw a figure. In response, Ron offered to help, but the interviewer said that it was his mother's turn to draw. When she finally managed to draw a man on her side of the page, her son praised her, but she

Figure 11.7 Leah and Ron complete a half drawing to create a whole drawing

interjected and said that she did not believe in her creative abilities, and continued drawing the ground, flowers, the sky, and the sun.

When they were asked about their experience during the exercise, both mother and son commented that they had a pleasant experience. Ron added that he felt embarrassed because he does not know how to draw. The mother replied that she was also embarrassed at the start of the process, but as she continued to draw, she started to enjoy the exercise, and that she enjoyed drawing as a child. When they discussed the mother's observation of her son when he was drawing, she commented that she was aware of his tendency to be precise and to draw within the lines. The son mentioned that he was disappointed that he did not draw any other details comparable to the ones his mother drew on her side, such as the sky or flowers. The mother then responded that she tried to complete the pastoral atmosphere in her son's drawing when he started to draw.

Comments about the Exercise

This exercise is suitable for children who have reached a developmental level that allows them to understand the presence of another person or position. When the child is unable to understand this concept, this exercise can be carried out on two separate sheets: the child draws freely on one page, and the parent tries to copy the child's drawing on a completely separate page.

This exercise is different from the previous exercises in this chapter. In the previous exercises, there was space for both the individual and the shared drawing where the partners drew together, but in this last exercise, the child leads the creative process and the parent is invited to try to "stand in the child's shoes." The central idea in this technique is attunement. It concerns the extent to which a parent can observe a child and the nuances of the creative process, and successfully complete (or copy when using the alternative technique) the drawing in the child's own style and in a way that characterizes his or her work. Parents who are able to do so accurately are able to enter the child's creative experience and attune themselves and gauge how the child feels when they draw with light or heavy pressure, in an open or closed manner, with an abstract or concrete theme. At the same time, the child can experience the parent's degree of attunement and witness the parent's attempt to understand the experience for the child as it was expressed in the drawing. This experience can unify the parent and child, as well as explore the differences between them, and help determine whether it is characterized by similarity or differences that most likely exist in other areas of their lives.

In the Leah and Ron example, when Leah attempted to complete her son's drawing and maintain the atmosphere that he started to create, there were areas in which her additional elements were not appropriate because she did not consider the drawing or was not attentive to what her son was creating. For example, she chose a different color for the ground in her drawing. The way she completed his drawing and emphasized sections that were missing in his work, for example when she only drew the sky in her section, or when she added oranges to his tree, possibly emphasized the differences between them and his problem of paying too much attention to details. This may have contributed to his feeling of dissatisfaction. In therapy, the pattern of responses would be discussed and defined, and connected to familiar patterns from everyday life to better understand their significance.

This exercise can be done with various art materials and art platforms. It would be interesting to observe what happens to a parent and child dyad who are used to working with specific materials and at a later stage are instructed to work with an art material that they are less familiar with. The therapist can engage the parent and child in a discussion about the artwork to enable them to voice what they felt during the various stages of work: how did the child feel when he or she was drawing and the parent was watching? How did the parent feel when observing the child? How did the child feel when he or she stopped and allowed the parent to continue the drawing? How did the parent feel when asked to continue the drawing? How did the child feel when he or she observed the parent complete the drawing? How did they feel and what were they thinking throughout the process, and in relation to the final product? This exercise can also be done in reverse order where the parent leads the process and begins the drawing and the child completes it.

Intervention 8: A Story between Two Drawings

Materials

Three A4 sheets of paper and two sets of markers.

Arrangement of the Therapy Room

The parent and child sit at the table apart from each other. The child and parent are each given a separate set of markers.

Instructions

The parent and child use the markers to draw freely on the page. It is important for them to work separately without being able to see each other's drawing (they can be at different tables). After they finish drawing, the parent and child show each other their drawings. In the next stage, they are asked to create a third drawing that links their two drawings and then tell a story that relates all three drawings.

Example

Yonat, aged 38, a mother of three children (including a baby just a few months old) drew with Adi, her 8-year-old middle daughter. They were each given a single A4 sheet of paper and a set of markers. The daughter responded with great enthusiasm at the sight of the markers: "Yeah, I love drawing with markers. Markers and gouache paints are my favorite." The mother and daughter were asked to sit at opposite ends of the table. The mother started drawing first and used two shades of green on the bottom of the page to draw stems and leaves (see Figure 11.8). She then added flowers in shades of pink and purple, and appeared very focused. Adi watched her mother draw for a few moments and then also started drawing. She drew the outline of brown mountains (see Figure 11.9). While she was drawing, she occasionally looked up at her mother's drawing and used similar colors (e.g., when she drew the grass and flowers) and similar images (such as clouds). When the mother announced that she had finished drawing, the daughter asked to see what she had made. After viewing her mother's drawing, the daughter continued to draw flowers slowly and carefully, and she seemed to enjoy being the center of attention. The daughter finished drawing approximately 15 minutes later.

When they worked together on the joint drawing (see Figure 11.10), the mother took a yellow marker, but waited for her daughter to join her. Adi told her: "You draw the grass, and I'll draw the stems, like you did in your drawing." The mother drew dark green grass and the daughter added yellow "inner layers of grass." This method of drawing created the same type of grass as in the mother's own drawing. The daughter continued giving her mother instructions, and the similarity of the joint drawing to the mother's own drawing slowly became evident. While they were working, the mother and daughter each hummed a different song. The only image that appeared in both the daughter's drawing and the joint drawing was the sun. At her mother's suggestion, Adi started telling a story about the three drawings: "There once was a sun that shone and then the flowers grew, and then the birds came and everybody played together." Afterwards, the interviewer asked Yonat to add something to the story: "It was a spring day, and the sky was clear," but her daughter rejected the mother's contribution to the story and said: "The sky wasn't clear, we didn't even draw the sky, we drew clouds."

Comments about the Exercise

Unlike the previous exercises, this exercise includes a narrative element that connects the individual parts to the joint section. This is intended to create a continuum between the separate sections. There is great potential for playfulness in this exercise. The parent and child may be surprised by each other's drawings, and the idea of creating a third drawing often

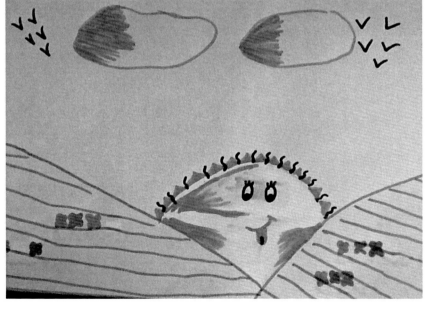

Figures 11.8–11.10 Yonat and Adi draw and tell a story between two drawings

leads to enjoyment and laughter. Similar to the previous exercises, this exercise encourages the transition between individual space and joint space. The transition is often not easy, and the work in the joint space may be accompanied by conflict over control, distance, and communication. It may also reveal issues that emerge when the parent and child deal with their difficulties in their relationship.

In the Yonat and Adi example, the daughter's need for a sense of control during the exercise dominated. She led the joint process and was unable to accept her mother's contribution to their story. At the same time, it was clear that she needed a mother who watched her. She wanted to take the "substance" that was embodied in her mother's images and perhaps wanted to please her mother and get closer to her in this way.

12 Family Exercises

Introduction

This chapter presents three exercises in which the parent and child are asked to create a visual representation of themselves and their families. In the first intervention technique, the parent and child draw the image of the child together. The second intervention technique involves a unique structured method where the parent and child draw themselves together on a joint page, and in the third technique, the parent and child create a collage composed of photographs taken from a family album. The three exercises provide a parent-child interactive experience based on creating a joint painting, much like the other exercises in this book. First and foremost, this type of interaction enables and promotes collaboration in a playful environment. Patterns of behavior that are representative of the relationship are given an outlet for expression. All the exercises constitute an opportunity for the parent and child to create a visual representation of the individuals within the relationship, and in two of the three exercises the relationship between individuals is also explored. The parent-child relationship emerges in all artwork, despite the fact that the pictorial representation can vary in the extent to which it appears to resembles the content.

Intervention 1: Following the Outline of the Body

Materials

Two sheets of cardboard, taped together to make one large sheet slightly larger than the height of the child, an HB pencil, a pencil sharpener and an eraser, gouache paints, paintbrushes, water jar, and rags.

Arrangement of the Therapy Room

The long sheet of cardboard is taped to the wall so that the bottom is level with the floor. Each participant is given a varied set of paintbrushes, a water jar, and a palette of gouache paints.

Instructions

The child stands with his or her back flush to the sheet of cardboard. The parent takes a pencil and slowly and carefully draws a line around the child's body. The parent is requested not to outline the child's private body parts (to refrain from drawing them). After the child steps away, parent and child can complete the missing sections of the body outline and correct any mistakes. Then, the parent and child color and fill in the body outline using the gouache paints since this material can be easily applied to cover large areas on the page. However, if they object to working with gouache paints, they can work with pastels. The parent and child are then asked to decide together how they would like to fill in the child's physical features and other details. In some situations, the therapist can suggest a drawing technique related to therapeutic objectives. One possibility is to attempt to paint the outline in a way that appears similar to the appearance of the child. Alternatively, the child can choose a costume and paint the outline to be wearing this costume (e.g., a dancer, a princess, a cowboy, etc.). The parent and child can also come up with their own guidelines for the drawing, or think of different work patterns depending on the therapeutic objectives. The sheet of cardboard can also be placed on the floor. In this position, the child can lie on top of the cardboard that can be folded in different ways, making the outline abstract and not necessarily following the child's shape accurately. If the parent and child decide to draw an abstract shape, they need to mutually decide the meaning and the nature of the character according to their individual and shared associations.

Example

Maha, aged 35, drew with Suheir, her daughter, who is 8 and a half years old. Suheir is the oldest child, is in third grade, and has a sister in kindergarten. The interviewer explained to Suheir that the tracing can be done with the cardboard pinned to the wall, or while she lies down on the sheet of cardboard in any position that she wants. After much deliberation, Suheir decided that she preferred drawing on the wall.

Then, Suheir contemplated how to stand next to the wall. The mother mentioned that there were a lot of possibilities and that she should decide which one she liked best. Suheir asked if she could stand in the same position as her mother did in her wedding picture in their living room at home. Her mother said yes. Suheir took this position on the wall, and her mother drew around her body with a pencil (see Plate 8).

When the outline was done, they both moved away from the wall and looked at the pencil lines. Suheir did not like the way her head was drawn, and her mother quickly reassured her and said that they could correct it. Suheir grabbed an eraser and wanted to erase this section of the drawing, but her mother asked her to wait until they drew it again before she erased any details. Suheir asked her mother to redraw her head, but this time she wanted her to draw it in profile. They then stepped back to the wall once again to look at the drawing, and Suheir's mother said she hoped she liked the outcome. The daughter replied that she was happy and that it looked much better. Suheir began to erase the initial outline of her face and her mother helped her.

In the next stage, the drawing was removed from the wall and placed on the floor so that mother and daughter could use the gouache paints. Suheir noticed that there was no skin color in the palette and asked why. The interviewer suggested that she mix colors together to make the color she wanted and she began to think what colors she would need to use to create a skin color. The mother asked her daughter whether she was considering painting the whole body without adding any clothes. The daughter laughed and replied that they would obviously add clothes, and the mother immediately started suggesting types of clothing. Suhair suggested she would draw pants down to the ankles, and a blouse that stopped at the elbow, so the remaining section of the arms would be painted a skin color. Suheir took a pencil and marked the clothing lines on the body and added a few small details to make the clothing special, such as buttons on the sleeves of the blouse and decorations on the belt. Suheir laughed when she noticed how the legs had been drawn since one was thicker than the other and her mother laughed with her. The mother asked Suheir what she should paint, and she said that she should start with the denim jeans. The mother attempted to mix colors together for the jeans, and her daughter suggested that she simply use blue and she would use black to create a textured look once she finished. Occasionally, Suheir turned to the interviewer and repeatedly asked her to join in their creative work. Suheir gave her mother very clear guidelines for the painting: she should be very consistent when coloring in the different sections, and if she decided to paint vertically on the one leg, she needed to do the same with the other. Suheir declared: "These are the rules of painting." At the same time, Suheir worked slowly and accurately to complete the belt. The mother worked on the legs and offered to make the narrow leg slightly wider and Suheir consented. Her mother finished painting the jeans and Suheir started creating the textured look. While she was painting, she asked her mother to paint the blouse pink and explained precisely how she wanted it done.

Suheir started working on the upper section and added a neck that connected the head to the body. She constantly made sure that her mother was working accurately and according to her strict guidelines. The mother mentioned that at her age, Suheir could afford to spend time on accuracy, which would not be possible after she gets married and has children. Suheir continued to guide her mother with great precision and instructed her how to create the skin color and how to paint the exposed areas of the body.

Later, she considered how to fill in the face, and she asked her mother to paint the eyes green because she wanted the eyes to be green just like hers were when she was little. She also requested blonde hair (Suheir has brown eyes and brown hair). Suheir started drawing the different parts of the face and her mother was very excited when she saw her daughter's drawing abilities. Maha helped Suheir draw, and if she made a mistake Suheir commented immediately. When Suheir accidently smudged the green from the eyes over the rest of the face, she blamed her mother, who in response quickly calmed her down. During the entire work process, Suheir was very strict about details. Her mother tried to draw accurately, and when she made a mistake Suheir reprimanded her, but this did not bother her or detract from her admiration for her daughter.

At the end of the work process, the interviewer hung the drawing on the wall, and they looked at it together for a few minutes. The mother was very enthusiastic about the work and said: "You wanted something similar to my wedding picture, and this is very close." The interviewer asked Suheir how she felt about the work. She did not answer immediately, and wanted to make it clear that one leg appeared thicker because she was wearing sweatpants. Maha continued to marvel at Suhair's drawing abilities. Suhair said she really liked cooperating with her mother and mentioned that it was different from drawing with a friend, because her mother was more supportive and empathetic. The mother said that it had been a long time since they had worked on a joint painting, and had the opportunity to observe and watch Suheir draw and add so many details without forgetting anything. The mother added that she was very proud of her daughter.

Comments about the Exercise

In this exercise, the parent and child are encouraged to create an image of the child together on the page. During the process, the subject of the child's self-image as seen by the child and by the parent is raised. In the example, the exercise elicited numerous aspects of the daughter's self-image and showed how differences in the mother and daughter's perceptions were reflected in the drawing. The joint symbolic references to the child's image on the page can be experienced as very enjoyable. The child can have the experience of being seen while drawing his or her image together with the parent—an image that reflects the real child as best as possible. The sincere effort to create a realistic representation of the child can be a pleasant and supportive experience. On the other hand, this process can reveal perceptions on the part of both parent and child in a less controlled and conscious manner. For example, a mother can attempt to organize and arrange a child's rougher sides that have been reflected in the drawing. The disparities between the participants' perceptions or reactions and their perceptions when they feel there are inaccuracies may make it possible to work on the internal representations of the relationship as they were expressed in these responses.

In the example with Suhair and Maha, the differences in their perceptions of Suhair's image, as well as various components of their relationship, could be observed. Suheir wanted to see herself as blonde and green-eyed. It was very important for her to work accurately and to produce a high-quality image. Both the mother and the daughter were concerned about the disparity between the way the legs were drawn. However, they were not able to correct this until the end of drawing process, and perhaps left a small part of their relationship for "lack of perfection." Suheir wanted her mother to be an extension of herself, and produce a character exactly the way that she wanted it to appear. She demanded a lot from herself and from her mother, and reprimanded her mother and was disappointed when things did not go exactly according to her plan. The mother tried her best to follow instructions, and although she did not have much leeway for independent decisions, she enjoyed seeing her daughter's abilities and continued to admire her work throughout the entire process. Another reoccurring motif in the creative process was the idea of what Suheir would like to be when she grows up: will she look like her mother on her wedding day? Will she be able to maintain her precision and high standards after she gets married and has children? The image of Suheir posing like her mother on her wedding day connected and linked their worlds.

Another variation on this exercise is to create a drawing that consists of costumes. In this type of drawing, there is a form of wish fulfillment that can empower the child, who can choose to be a powerful superhero such as Superman, or beautiful and elegant like a princess. The third variation on this exercise when the sheet of cardboard is folded on the floor enables a greater space for internal projections, which are facilitated by simply presenting a more abstract image. In this case, the inner parts of the self and perceptions about the child are easier to access. This exercise tends to produce elements of surprise and laughter that emerge during the creative process.

Intervention 2: Drawing the Parent and the Child in Sections

Materials

Two oval-shaped pieces of paper cut to the size of a human head, oil pastels, one and a half sheets of cardboard paper glued together to form a work surface, masking tape, gouache paints, paintbrushes, rags, a water jar, and other painting utensils.

Arrangement of the Therapy Room

The parent and child sit next to each other at the table. The two oval-shaped pieces of paper and sets of oil pastels are placed in front of them. Elsewhere in the room, the sheets of cardboard are taped to the wall and some gouache paints are placed next to them.

Instructions

The two participants are asked to use the oil pastels to draw their faces on the oval-shaped pieces of paper. Each participant draws his or her own face. At the end of the process, they are able to discuss the face they made and the feelings that emerged. Then, the participants tape the heads to the sheet of cardboard on the wall. They can change the location of their faces until they are both satisfied with the composition. Next, the participants are asked to work together on the joint sheet of cardboard and create bodies for the heads and an appropriate background for the drawing with gouache paints.

Example

Eli, aged 30, drew with his 6-year-old son, Nadav. Eli is a kindergarten teacher and a father of three. Nadav is his second child. Nadav asked his father what to do in the exercise and his father explained to him that he needed to draw a face. He then asked Nadav what features appear on a face. Nadav asked his father what color his eyes were, learned that they were brown, and then announced that he would be drawing a purple nose (see Figure 12.1). Eli asked Nadav what color he should paint his nose and Nadav answered that the nose is skin-colored, but he could draw it in any color he wanted. Later, Nadav declared that he had finished his drawing and his father reminded him that he also had to draw the ears and hair. Once again, Nadav checked with his father and asked what color his hair was. They agreed that his hair is black. Eli mentioned that he was going to draw a blue tongue and blonde hair. Nadav objected and told him that his hair is also black, but his father responded that he was creating an imaginary drawing. Eli finished the face drawing before Nadav and picked up his drawing and asked Nadav for his opinion. Nadav approved and continued to draw. A moment later, Nadav said that the mouth that he drew was too small and his father told him he could make it bigger if he did not like it. Then, Nadav began discussing colors with his father and asked how to draw ears, and his father encouraged him with support and admiration when he drew these details. They continued to talk about their facial features and remembered that they had to draw a chin. The father decided to add a chin and a throat. Nadav commented: "It was great! I tried to remember all the parts of the face and make it look like myself." His father replied: "I drew a face with imaginary colors. I felt like using funny colors. I had a lot of fun drawing this. I enjoyed it. I like to draw with nonrealistic colors, colors that make me happy."

In the next stage, the father taped the two face drawings to the cardboard on the wall. He consulted with Nadav where to place them and at what angle, and he followed Nadav's instructions so that basically Nadav decided where each drawing should be placed. Then they poured colors onto the palette. Eli checked with Nadav whether he knew what happened when different colors are mixed together. Nadav responded that he didn't know, and Eli replied: "Oh dear [jokingly], how can you go to school if you don't know?" The father began to explain to Nadav how the paints mix together and also how to rinse the paintbrush when changing colors. He also brought a chair for Nadav to stand on and advised him to start working with the thicker paintbrush. Nadav painted the sky and his father added an orange sun. Nadav stood on the chair and asked his father to bring him some more colors, to wet the paintbrush for him, and so on. When Nadav finished painting, he got off the chair and began to work on the grass on the lower section of the page. His father continued working on the upper section and added a face to the sun and a green tree. He said again that each of them was free to create whatever they wanted. Nadav added a bird to the drawing, but he was not satisfied with it. Eli told him that he could draw whatever he wanted, but if he was not satisfied, he could wipe it off. Nadav eagerly drew a flock of birds and his father was very impressed. The father added fruit to the tree and offered to draw clouds in the sky. Nadav suggested adding a road to their drawing and started painting it. Eli started painting his body and drew a black body with pink hands. He then suggested that they both take a few steps back and look at the drawing together. After viewing the drawing from afar, Nadav decided he wanted to add oranges to the tree. Nadav then focused on his character, and also colored the body black. His father reminded him that he did not have to color and paint like he did. Nadav added pink and yellow hands to the body and then decided to draw houses on the page. He often walked toward the balcony to look through the window to see what the houses outside looked like. In the end, they both laughed and posed for photographs with their drawing. While observing their drawing, the father noted that Nadav's figure was taller in the drawing and Nadav commented that he was also thinner. Nadav said that in the drawing: "Dad and Nadav are crossing the road when the green light for pedestrians is on." He added that it was fun to draw with his father. The father mentioned that he enjoyed the exercise very much and that it was their first time drawing together on the same page. He said he tried to urge Nadav not to use ordinary colors and enjoyed watching him go back and forth to the balcony to look for creative ideas that were not inside the room. Eli asked Nadav why he decided to make himself appear taller and Nadav

Figure 12.1 Eli and Nadav creating the parent and the child drawing in
sections

answered that he would be the father: "Because it's fun to be the father,
I want to be the father for a few days." Eli said that the most important
thing during the exercise was to make sure that Nadav understood that
the drawing does not have to mirror reality.

Comments about the Exercise

Similar to the other exercises described in this chapter, this exercise enables
the parent and child to create a visual representation of themselves and
their relationship. The exercise refers to the relationship during the work
process itself via the interaction between the participants as they draw and
their representations on the page. These elements can elicit issues such as
closeness versus distance, togetherness versus separation, leadership, and
control. At the end of this exercise and while observing their final work, the
therapist can ask the participants a number of questions concerning their
abilities to work as partners: what did they think of the exercise? Where

were the drawings of the heads placed in relation to each other on the page? Was there room for both partners on the page? What did the differences in size and position say about the relationship between the characters? Was there any contact between the characters? Were they separate? Did they overlap? Did each participant maintain his or her personal boundaries? Did each participant feel comfortable with the place and position of the characters? What characterized the process in terms of decision-making, authority, and support as opposed to conflict?

The Eli and Nadav example illustrates a joint painting exercise where the father and son collaborated. Eli encouraged Nadav to go on a colorful adventure where everything was possible and there was plenty of room for humor. Nadav was also willing to explore and convey elements from the real world (what he saw from the balcony) and from his imagination and from his wishes (where he is the father and the father is the son) into their drawing. The father occasionally took a didactic approach (by teaching Nadav how to mix colors and listing the different parts of the face), but he quickly made sure to disconnect from reality and urged his son to do the same to continue their joint journey. The experience was fun for both of them.

Intervention 3: Pictures from Family Life

Materials

The parent and child are asked to bring copies of family photographs from home that they can work on together in the exercise. The family can print the pictures in advance or photocopy them. The exercise also requires a quarter or a half sheet of cardboard, a glue stick, colored pencils, and oil pastels.

Arrangement of the Therapy Room

The parent and child sit at the table next to each other. The sheet of cardboard is placed in front of them, along with their pictures and the drawing materials. If there is a photocopy machine in the room, the participants can enlarge the pictures or specific sections of the pictures if they wish.

Instructions

There are a number of variants to this exercise framework:

1   The parent and child are asked to select one photograph that they relate to, and try to draw it together on the cardboard.
2   The parent and child work with an enlarged version of a photograph and color it with the pencils or crayons of their choice.
3   The parent and child are asked to create a collage from a variety of photographs of their family life. They choose which photographs are more important than others, where to place each one, and how to connect them.

Example

Meital, 33, drew with Tal, her oldest son, aged 10 and a half. Meital is a kindergarten teacher and the mother of three children. She sat down to work with Tal, while her youngest son, a 16-month-old, sat on her lap. After the instructions were given, the mother selected pictures by herself and suggested that they start by cutting up the photographs. Tal reminded her that there were several ways to do the exercise, but the mother had already decided that they would make a joint collage (see Figure 12.2). Tal said he had problems with using glue and his mother told him to cut the pictures and she would paste them onto the cardboard. The mother suggested that they should first lay out the pictures before gluing them to decide together which ones to include in the collage. While she was cutting up the pictures, the baby on Meital's lap began interfering with their work process by trying to touch various objects. Meital suggested that they place the pictures in the center of the page and create a border with a mosaic of colored blocks. She said: "You and I will complete this section quickly and then you can paint flowers and the sky on the page." Tal did not like the idea, but eventually went along with his mother. Meital looked for bright pieces of paper and asked Tal if he wanted to use one color or many. Tal decided that they would use different colors. He was constantly distracted by the television in the background and accidently dropped the colored sheets that his mother brought him because he was watching. Metial reprimanded him and reminded him again that it would be better "to talk less and work more." She began to spread glue on the page and asked Tal to place the mosaic blocks along the border. Because Tal was dawdling, his mother warned him that if he did not start working immediately, he would have to do his homework instead. Tal arranged the mosaic blocks according to color and his mother praised him. He worked for a little longer and then said that he did not want to go on. His mother persuaded him to start working again, and in the end he agreed. Meanwhile, his mother stopped pasting the colorful blocks to tend to her baby. When they finally finished gluing the mosaic border, they admired their joint effort and seemed happy together. Then, mother and son began to work with the pictures. It was obvious that Tal was not interested in continuing the joint work, and he started to whine and complain, but he reluctantly agreed to arrange the pictures while his mother pasted them. After this phase, Meital asked her son how he would like to decorate their work. Tal did not want to continue working and they continued discussing the matter together. In the end, Tal decided he would draw a rainbow and showed his mother how to draw one. The mother suggested that they work together, but Tal refused and only agreed to work taking turns. When Meital tried to work with him, he immediately prevented her from drawing and reminded her that they were working in turns. Tal was satisfied with what he had created on the page, and his mother said that it was pretty, but she wouldn't have used the color brown. They continued talking, and the mother leisurely commented: "We are so bad at this." The discussion was casual and

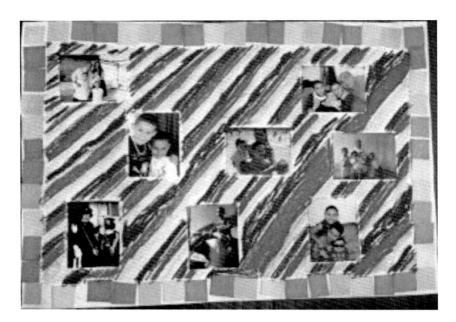

Figure 12.2 Meital and Tal work with pictures from family life (photos have been obscured for anonymity)

accompanied by laughter on both sides. Tal noted that the red section he painted was very thick, and therefore the biggest. He then added that his mother should use thin lines. His mother responded that she had no problem coloring thin lines since the little ones have nothing to worry about. Tal replied that they do have things to worry about—sometimes little ones are afraid at the movies, but that he is also afraid, and that adults also have fears. In the end, both mother and son said that they enjoyed working together and that their artwork was pretty.

Comments about the Exercise

In this exercise, the creation of a visual representation of the relationship is characterized by less psychological distance than in the previous exercises. The emphasis is on actual family members, whereas in many other exercises the aim is to better understand the nature of the parent-child relationship as elicited through symbolic objects and images that are more detached. Each variation of the exercise has a slightly different feature that gives the participants a slightly different experience. In the first variation, in which participants are asked to copy a larger version of a photograph onto the page, interpretations can be based on identifying specific areas that were emphasized, forgotten, spaces that were changed, boundaries that were added, and so on. These modifications are usually made unconsciously, and observing them can reveal hidden aspects of the relationship. In the second variation, in which the participants color an enlarged photocopy of a family photograph, the original photograph serves as a basis that to some extent contains and directs the creative approach. Different aspects of the relationship are revealed in the way that the partners color in the picture in relation to the original photograph, and the different sections within the photograph. In the third variation, where the partners prepare a joint collage, the parent and child consciously decide how they would like to design and create their family photograph. The cutting process, the ability to enlarge the images, and the ability to paste and draw promote the creation of an imaginary and playful world that can often be entertaining and funny. Similar to other joint drawings, in this exercise, aspects of closeness, intimacy, independence, and control can be observed. In all three variations of the exercise, and when the creative process is complete, the participants can observe the final product and discuss how they feel about the final product. They can also explore the relationship between the parent and child as it was reflected in the work, as well as the relationships with the rest of the family members as presented in the collage.

In the Meital and Tal exercise, the intricacy of the joint painting experience emerged in the way that the mother selected the pictures on her own. Tal was not involved in the selection process at all, and there was no discussion about the pictures or their significance for either the mother or the son. In this example, the mother was focused on completing the task and involved Tal in something he may not have liked (and perhaps she also did not like). There were also many distractions in the room during the creative process, including from the baby on the mother's lap who wanted a great deal of attention and interfered with the participants' activities. Despite the distractions, two interesting developments took place during the exercise: first, the joint work created a space where Tal could speak openly with his mother about his inner world and his concerns and fears, despite the lack of a therapeutic setting. It is hard to determine whether this type of conversation would have taken place under different circumstances. Second, despite their problems synchronizing, the mother and son had moments of laughter and experiences of "togetherness." They both left the session with a sense of enjoyment.

13 An Encounter in the Interpersonal Space

Introduction

This chapter, which is the last in the section that presents clinical intervention techniques, presents three exercises for the parent and child in a joint drawing space. These intervention techniques provide a particularly intimate encounter that sometimes leads to the blurring of interpersonal boundaries and can spark fun and playfulness. Much like the techniques that have been addressed thus far, the joint interactive spaces facilitate types of encounters that differ in terms of their levels of cooperation, models of leadership, and the way in which participants relate to each other. The first intervention technique consists of a joint painting created by both the parent and child, the second intervention technique involves working with a tray and a marble where the partners' joint movements create the final product, and in the third intervention technique both participants are taken on a colorful adventure where their feet serve as the painting tools, and they create artwork together on a sheet of paper spread out on the floor. It is important to emphasize that these three exercises guide the parent and child to engage in experiences that may enable them to merge, oftentimes creating a space in which it is not clear where one individual begins and the other continues. It is crucial to make sure that the intervention technique is appropriate for the specific parent-child dyad and that it integrates well into their therapeutic process.

Intervention 1: Working Together without Verbal Communication

Materials

A half or full sheet of cardboard, two sets of oil pastels, two sets of gouache paints, paintbrushes, water jars, and rags. Regardless of the chosen material, both participants should work with the same material. Each participant is given a separate but identical set of colors.

Arrangement of the Therapy Room

The cardboard is preferably attached to the wall horizontally, and the art work is carried out by standing next to the wall. The painting materials are placed alongside each participant. If this is not possible, the parent and child sit next to each other at a table with the sheet of cardboard placed horizontally in front of them on the table.

Instructions

The therapist explains to both the parent and child that the exercise is conducted without speaking. The partners can draw whatever they feel like on the cardboard. The drawing can be figurative or abstract. At the end of the work, another cardboard sheet should be given to them to make a new drawing following the same instructions.

Example

Inbal, 32, drew with her oldest daughter, May, who is 8 years old. Inbal is married with three children. In the first drawing (see Figure 13.1), the mother and daughter worked while sitting together at the table. After the presentation of the exercise, May said how pleased she was to work with oil pastels. She added that she had been dreaming of having these art materials, but her mother was not willing to buy them for her. Her mother reminded May that the exercise required them not to speak to each other. Inbal began drawing the central figure (she started by drawing the outline of the figure's dress) while her daughter watched her, but did not join in. Then, she added a body to the figure and began filling the figure with a flesh color. The daughter picked up different pastels several times but did not start drawing. Finally, she began to draw a thick, brown tree trunk and then said that she had no idea what to draw and that her tree was not good. Her mother responded by saying that it was not a test, and it did not need to be good, and then added: "Mine is not good either." Inbal sat upright and concentrated on her drawing, while her daughter bent over the drawing, sitting cross-legged and almost lying down on the sheet. Inbal continued to work on the figure of the woman her daughter added leaves and fruit to the tree. She then drew clouds and her daughter added a sky above. During the work process, the mother and daughter worked in turns. The daughter added an umbrella to the figure and then the mother added ground to the landscape of the drawing. Her daughter watched her as she drew. They continued to work in turns: the daughter added rain and lightning, the mother added another tree on the right side of the page, the daughter drew apples falling from the tree and added a few apples that had fallen to the ground under two trees, and the mother drew stubby flowers bunched between the first tree and the figure. After they completed the work, May inquired if she was allowed to write something. She labeled the first tree "Ordinary apples," and next to the mother's tree she wrote "Pink Lady apples," and then she said: "These are the good apples." The mother added another tree on the left side of the page, a tree that was not a fruit tree. The daughter added a flower that was much larger than the other flowers that faced the figure and touched one of its hands. The mother and daughter joined together to draw the bushes while sharing colors with each other. At the end, both the mother and daughter looked at each other and announced with a smile: "We're done." After completing the drawing, May commented: "A few days ago in class, we drew 'The Giving Tree' in honor of Tu Bishvat [the Jewish New Year for the trees], and today I continued with the same drawing, and later when Mom drew, I wanted to connect with her idea. Mom did most of the drawing." Her mother replied: "You are not exaggerating at all [ironically] . . . You did this and this and this . . . [she points them out]. Occasionally, I created the outlines and you painted inside and added other elements—thunder, rain, an umbrella. I started to draw a woman and I noticed that May was drawing a tree, and at that stage I didn't know what she was trying to draw. When I saw that she was adding more natural elements to the drawing, I followed her idea."

After their conversation, May added a speech bubble to the character and wrote inside: "I am cold," and said: "It's scary that she is wearing shorts outside because it's raining." The mother added a scarf to the figure and May drew a bag of apples that the figure had picked

Figure 13.1 Inbal and May working together without verbal communication

and wrote: "Free apples." At the end, May added a black line between
the figure and the tree and said: "You need to add a fence for apple-
picking so it will be a safe place." May spoke and summed up their
drawing experience: "My mom had the idea. She started drawing and
I developed with her—we progressed like a mother and daughter, and
we moved together. It's mutual. Sometimes I lead and then she leads.
It's like taking turns when you play hide and seek . . . In the drawing,
it's mom who is in the rain and who is going to the supermarket to buy
and prepare me my favorite dish—apples."

In the second drawing (see Figure 13.2), Inbal took a purple pastel and
May selected a gray one. The daughter drew a rectangle on the right side
of the page and her mother drew two semicircles in the top left corner.
The daughter turned the rectangle into a building. The mother added an
orange fence next to the building and the daughter joined her and colored
the fence red. Afterwards, Inbal and May added purple curtains to the
house, and the mother drew a red and brown slide. May then added a sandbox, a house with a red roof, a sun with a face, blue curtains, and park play
structures. The mother added a tree, green curtains, more houses, and a
swing. The daughter drew a large purple bird and three smaller pink birds
that touched one another. The mother drew a boy with a ball and May
drew a girl. Once again, the mother sat upright, while her daughter was
physically close to her, bent over, and almost leaning on her. The mother
made it clear that she was finished working and sat back comfortably.
The daughter continued to draw and added figures and other details. The
mother watched her daughter and they both started laughing. When they
finished the drawing, May said: "I drew a building and houses and sand
[a sandbox in the park] so that the children playing in the garden will have
a soft landing. I made a mother bird and three little birds. The girl in the
drawing is the Swiss girl at my school. My inspiration came from the girls
in her class who think that they are beauty queens and want to be models,
so I tried to show this in the drawing, but it doesn't look so good." Her
mother added: "I tried to draw something purple and I wasn't sure what it
was, but I saw that she had drawn a building so I joined her and eventually
we created an entire neighborhood."

At the end of the process, the mother and daughter talked about the
differences between their two drawings. May said: "The experience was
different. At first [in the first drawing], I didn't know what to do, and in
this one I had an inspiration. Here, I added things I wanted to add there,
but only now there was room for them. I feel better. Relief. It was hard for
me in the first one and easy for mom, and now it was the opposite." The
mother responded: "It's true, the first one was easier and here it was more
difficult. At the beginning [of the second drawing], I wanted to create an
abstract drawing, but I went with her idea. I could have left it alone and
let us both drawing two different things, but I wanted a guideline. I love
that it's connected. The first one was easier because I approached the page

Figure 13.2 Inbal and May working together without verbal communication

and started drawing, and everything could be connected, and I find it hard when it's not homogenous, and here I drew something that was not clear and hers seemed like a better idea, so I went with it."

Comments about the Exercise

Working on a joint painting without the use of words is one of the basic techniques of art therapy. This technique offers the parent and child an opportunity to renounce their familiar space of verbal communication, and create a nonverbal form of interaction with the use of colors that can be recorded on the page. In this way, nonverbal representations and hidden aspects within the relationship, together with typical characteristics of the interaction, are reflected on the page. Due to the less familiar nature of the joint space, the participants have less control over what they express, and unconscious content may be expressed. The joint painting can serve as a space for the shared observation of the parent and child, or for the parent during the parent training sessions. In this space, the existing patterns within the relationship are observed, but at the same time there is an opportunity for change. For example, the drawing space can give the child the opportunity to change his or her natural tendency to cling to the parent, and draw more independently.

According to the stage in the therapeutic process, and when the drawing is complete, the therapist can suggest to the parent and child to observe the final artwork and review and recount the creative process. This review process can reveal where each one of the partners is situated on the page, who led and who followed, to what extent they expressed themselves in the joint painting, what images emerged and their significance in the context of the relationship, how they felt at the end of the drawing experience, and the differences or similarities between the two drawings, if any. This review process helps to define feelings that arise in the relationship, perceptions of the self and the other, types of behavior, expectations from the other regarding the relationship, and so on, as they are reflected on the page. In the next stage, and depending on the therapeutic process, the therapist can help the parent and child to create some form of a connection between the recognized patterns in the drawings and those in real life outside the therapy room.

It is recommended to give the parent and child two drawing exercises, one after the other. The first drawing often serves as an introductory platform to the media and the transition to nonverbal forms of communication, as well as a "warm-up" exercise, much like it was for May in this example. After this first encounter, and when the partners draw on the second page, they may find that it is possible to communicate better, learn from the previous drawing experience, and implement what was learned, and as such create a change in the new space. However, in some instances, the transition to the second drawing may expose internal content and parts of the relationship that were "contained" or hidden in the first drawing.

Finally, therapists are often inclined to permit free interaction during the joint drawing process to allow the partners to express the relationship as it is, including its qualities and difficulties. However, in specific parent-child dyads, it is advisable to consider the fit between the therapeutic objectives and the instructions for the exercise. For example, there may be certain parent-child drawing interactions where the therapist prohibits participants from drawing on each other's drawing because this particular issue was previously addressed in therapy and the joint painting process may allow for a change in this pattern of behavior.

In Inbal and May's drawings, they initially each drew on the half of the page that was closer to each of them, and in both cases the mother was the one who initiated cooperation between the sections, and the daughter accepted her invitation. In the first drawing, the initial images converged into one scene, but in the second drawing the mother did not proceed in her own direction and worked according to May's theme. The mother and daughter did not exchange many glances, but occasionally exchanged giggles, and there were significant moments of closeness during the creative process. It was hard for the daughter not to speak, and this was openly expressed when she asked to add words to the drawing. Throughout the entire work process, there were transitions between working together and working in turns where one worked and the other observed. In relation to the images, the daughter addressed the mother in "admiration"—she said that the mother's figure was beautiful and the mother's apples were the good ones. The daughter added autobiographical elements to both drawings: in the first drawing, this appeared in the way the mother depicted her favorite food, and in the second drawing there was a mother bird with her three children and a child from school. The mother preferred to relate to more general scenes.

Intervention 2: A Tray and a Marble

Materials

Several sheets of A3 paper, gouache paints, a few glass marbles (preferably large ones), and a large baking tray.

Arrangement of the Therapy Room

The parent and child stand facing each other. The baking tray is placed on the table between them and the gouache paints are diluted slightly with water.

Instructions

First, the therapist asks the parent and child to pour the diluted gouache paints into the tray, and place the marbles inside the tray as well. Then, the parent and child each hold two corners of the tray and tilt it back and forth so that the marbles roll around in the different colors. Please note: if the gouache is too watery, the colors will instantly mix and merge into one dollop of fluid, but if the paint is too thick, it will be difficult to get the marbles to move on the tray. When the paint is diluted to the right density, the movements of the marbles create colorful and interesting patterns in the tray. Next, the tray is placed on the table, and a series of prints is made by carefully placing and submerging A3 pages into it. Last, the participants observe the prints and each selects one print to work with individually and freely, or tries to define an image within the print using gouache paints.

Example

Anat, 35, drew with her 6-year-old daughter, Yael. First, they were given the instructions for the exercise and could choose as many colors as they wanted and pour them into the tray wherever they chose. Anat asked her daughter what colors she wanted to use and Yael very quietly answered

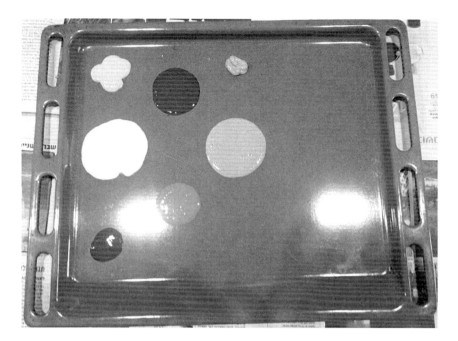

Figure 13.3 Anat and Yael drawing with a tray and a marble

that she would like to work with pink and turquoise. The mother handed the bottle of pink paint to her daughter and asked her to pour the turquoise paint into the tray. Yael then pointed at different colors that she wanted to use, and her mother handed them to her and she poured them into the tray. In the end, the mother suggested that they pour all the colors into the tray (see Figure 13.3).

Then, the mother and her daughter were each given a marble and they were asked to place them anywhere on the tray. Each of them held two corners of the tray and together moved the marbles and watched them slide through different colors. They worked together and expressed their enjoyment of the exercise (see Figure 13.4). They quietly tried to slide the marble through every color and voiced expressions of wonder and amazement.

Anat asked Yael what she thought about the end product, and Yael answered that it looked good. Then, the interviewer handed them several sheets of A3 paper to imprint the patterns in the tray. The mother and her daughter pressed the pages down onto the colors and Yael moved her hand over the top of the page to add pressure. When they peeled away the pages from the tray, they both admired the outcome. They then took the next page, and the mother suggested that they create a print in which they

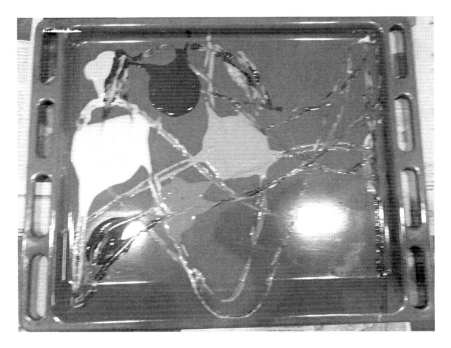

Figure 13.4 Anat and Yael drawing with a tray and a marble

smeared the colors together. Anat pointed out that every print was different and repeatedly asked her daughter if she thought they were good.

Finally, the mother and daughter each chose a print and were told they could draw and add colors to the print. The mother poured out some gouache paints for them to use and the daughter began to smear the colors in her drawing (see Figure 13.5). The mother started creating a red heart on her print. The daughter watched her mother and inquired if she was allowed to draw on only one page. The mother immediately asked her if she was not satisfied with what she had made, and offered her another sheet. The daughter took the new sheet and began to draw a red heart like her mother had drawn (see Figure 13.6). The mother then added a blue heart, turquoise birds, and a yellow sun (see Figure 13.7). Yael looked at Anat's drawing, and Anat said to her: "You know you don't have to do exactly what I do, you can do whatever you want. You can draw the same things as I have drawn, or you can draw whatever you want. You draw very well." Yael continued to watch her mother draw and added a sun to her drawing. The mother wrote the word "LOVE" on her drawing and her daughter used similar colors to draw on her page. Yael added a butterfly and the mother quickly responded: "Amazing! I never thought of that [the butterfly]. Wow, sweetie . . . It's perfect." They continued to draw in silence until the end of the exercise, and the mother commented on her daughter's drawing and said: "It's great, sweetie."

During the conversation after they completed the drawing, Yael felt very embarrassed and asked her mother to switch drawings with her. With much effort, Yael said quietly that she had fun and she drew hearts, butterflies, and flowers. Her mother continued to encourage her to speak and describe the work process. The mother asked questions and Yael answered quietly and hesitantly. Yael said that her favorite part of the exercise was the drawing. Anat said she most enjoyed working with the marbles because she did this part together with her daughter. The mother said she was somewhat embarrassed because her daughter felt so shy during the session. The mother did not give up and continued to ask her daughter about every part of the drawing. Yael loved the color yellow that was like the sun, the blue that was like the swimming pool that she loves, the red heart because of her love for her mother, and the butterflies just because they can fly. She said that in her mother's drawing, she loved the hearts and butterflies, and Anat corrected her that they are in fact birds. The mother said: "I loved the strong colors, because after we created the prints, the colors faded. I then chose the drawing that had the strongest colors. I drew hearts because I felt closer to Yael while we were drawing and I love her. I drew the hearts for her, and the sun because she is my sunshine." The mother then commented about Yael's drawing: "It's stunning. My favorite part is the butterfly that

Figure 13.5 Anat and Yael drawing with a tray and a marble: the daughter's first drawing

Figure 13.6 Anat and Yael drawing with a tray and a marble: the daughter's second drawing

Figure 13.7 Anat and Yael drawing with a tray and a marble: the mother's drawing

she drew so very beautifully. In my opinion, it's perfect." In the end, the mother said that Yael really loves to draw but this was hard for them both. She added: "The page was full and it was hard for me to connect to the drawing itself and create another drawing out of it. When you get a blank page, you draw whatever you like from start to finish. A complete drawing. When you get a page that contains something else, you need to adjust yourself to the drawing and this was a bit more challenging for me."

Comments about the Exercise

The various stages of the exercise offer several encounters in the interpersonal space. Moving the marbles inside the tray encourages the partners to be together in a completely joint space. There is no space for "me" and "you." Every movement inside the tray is the result of the joint movement of the tray, and therefore every trace made by the marble is a shared creation. In many ways, this is similar to a symbiotic experience in which two beings are experienced as one. In this context, the blurring of boundaries can be experienced as a positive and constructive experience, because it allows for the creation of a positive and esthetic product in a situation where there is cooperation and the absence of leadership. This stage is very important on the experiential level, and in our opinion the mere presence of the other person in this stage of the work can be of value to the parent and child.

The stage of creating the prints maintains, captures, and therefore validates the existence of the joint space. It also facilitates the progression to the final stage of the exercise, in which each participant connects to him or herself again, to the personal images and attempts to deal with the space independently through the processing of the prints. According to psychoanalytic theory, the ability to endure a transition between togetherness and individuality is very important in terms of creating satisfactory personal relationships (Solan, 1991).

The discussion after the drawing phase in this exercise may encourage the parent and child to share their experiences during each stage of the work process, and particularly their thoughts in the transition between working together and working individually. Depending on the stage of the therapeutic process, the therapist can propose a connection between the content that was expressed in the drawing and the creative process, and the content that surfaced in the relationship.

In Anat and Yael's work, it was possible to observe how well suited they were for the joint work stage, in which they moved the marbles around the tray. This stage was playful and enjoyable, and the mother even commented that it was the stage that she most enjoyed. However, during the printing stage of the exercise, in which there was once again space for separation, Yael struggled to separate from her mother and tried to produce a drawing that was identical to the one her mother had created. It was very clear that Anat found it difficult to see Yael struggle to separate from her and find her own place on the printed page. Yael associated this struggle to her experience of coping with a sheet of paper that was full, but it is evident that being alone, specifically after a significant stage of working together, was not easy for Yael.

Intervention 3: Walking in Gouache Paints

Materials

Eight 240g cardboard sheets of paper, a roll of masking tape, gouache paints, a bucket with warm water, and a towel.

Arrangement of the Therapy Room

The therapist, or the therapist together with the parent and child, tape the eight cardboard sheets of paper together to create a cardboard "carpet" on the floor. There is a chair, a bucket of warm water, and a towel next to the "carpet." Several bottles of gouache paints are placed directly on the "carpet." A number of different colors can be used, each of them separately in different places on the "carpet." The participants' clothes should be covered and protected, and preferably they should bring clothes that can get dirty (an apron will not be helpful since participants often work when kneeling on the "carpet").

Instructions

For this exercise, there are several work techniques that can be used depending on the therapeutic objectives. One possibility is for the parent and child to remove their shoes, dip their feet in the gouache paints, walk on the "carpet," and create footprints. Alternatively, only the child walks on the carpet and the parent serves as an anchor and supports the child from outside the carpet. This situation makes it easier to avoid slipping and falling, and many colors can be used. While the parent holds the child's hand, the child can gently slide along the paint.

Example

Yael, 31, drew with Eden, her 7-year-old daughter. At the time, Yael was in the process of separating from her husband. Eden is the middle daughter between her two brothers. The mother described Eden as having a rough time as a result of her parents' separation. The mother awaited the session in the hope that a creative activity could help her daughter cope with everyday events.

At the beginning of the session, Eden helped prepare the cardboard carpet and preferred to tape the sheets together. Two options were presented to Yael and Eden—to walk and create a painting together on the carpet, or have Eden walk on the carpet alone while the mother supported her from the side. The daughter chose the second option. The mother was glad that she would not get covered in paint. Eden wanted to create the color pink, and the mother asked her if she remembered what colors she had to mix together to get pink. Eden remembered and poured red and white paint together onto the carpet. Her mother supported her as she stepped on the paint and made sure she did not slip. Eden asked her mother to pull her along the carpet so she could slide as though she was skiing along the surface (see Figures 13.8 and 13.9). The two of them laughed and mixed more paint, and then repeated the sliding action. Afterwards, Eden wanted to make purple, and her mother suggested that she add blue to the pink paint on the carpet. Her daughter was not satisfied at first with the color that she made, and added more red and blue paint until she was satisfied and continued to slide with the colors. When there was not enough paint to allow her to slide on the carpet, she added yellow to the other colors. The mother warned her that it would become brown, but at that point the daughter simply wanted to keep sliding on the paints, regardless of their color. She continued sliding around the page with all the colors until one of the sides of the pages tore, and she moved to the other side of the carpet. She poured the three primary colors onto the page and mixed them together using her feet while her mother held her hands. She then continued sliding. This was accompanied by giggles, great joy, as well as moments of confidence juxtaposed with moments of panic for fear of falling, and then more laughter. Eden added black to the puddle of paint and it was no longer possible to identify any specific color on the carpet. The paint had already oozed onto the floor, but it did not seem to matter to the mother or the child.

Then, Eden began to walk on the paints that were already starting to dry and she enjoyed the feeling of her feet sticking to the paper. The mother turned on some Purim music (a Jewish holiday), and suggested that they might as well play music in the background if they were dancing. The mother and daughter poured more color combinations onto the carpet, with the sole purpose of allowing the daughter to continue to slide on the paint, regardless of the shades that were created. After 40 minutes of playing with the paints, the daughter washed her feet in the bucket while her mother held her hands, but when she stepped out of the bucket she wanted to return to the paints and not stop the exercise. The mother suggested that they dance on the carpet to the sound of one more song and then she would go and take a shower. Eden had a big smile on her face and agreed.

The two partners continued to dance for the duration of one more song. At the end of the song, the daughter sat down on the carpet and spread out her arms and legs on the paints. The mother began to photograph her and enjoyed seeing her daughter act so freely with the paints, and commented that it was more difficult for her to let go in the same way. At the end of the exercise, the mother's legs were covered with paint because Eden had slid in her direction throughout the creative process and paint had splashed

Figures 13.8–13.9 Yael and Eden walking in gouache paints

on her. Eden was totally covered in paint except for her face. When Eden finished playing on the carpet, she washed her feet in the bucket while leaning on her mother, and walked over to the shower, leaving colorful footprints behind her.

Comments about the Exercise

The action of painting with one's feet and creating gouache prints on paper is a special, rare experience, and therefore particularly enjoyable for many clients. The parent and child can create colorful and interesting joint art-work with their feet and experience a great sense of freedom, ease, and spontaneity, particularly in comparison to the regular, familiar art exer-cises using one's hands. Therefore, this type of exercise allows for many different encounters on the page, where the partners cover and work on top of each other's creations to make an esthetic and colorful end product. The potential for a sense of freedom and enjoyment of the creative process intensifies when the child slides on the paint. The parent supports the child through a regressive process as the child undergoes a primary sensori-motor experience. The parent's support simulates forms of earlier parental support in the child's life during stages of holding and touching. In this way, the process can complete or allow for an experience that was absent during the child's early development.

In the Yael and Eden example, the exercise was particularly significant because of their family situation. Yael's ability to allow Eden to be in an open and accepting space, even though she was getting dirty, helped Eden to confidently enter the regressive experience while knowing that her mother, as in everyday life, would accompany and support her, and would be there for her if she fell. At the beginning of the exercise, Eden was focused on blending the colors, but as the creative process progressed, she sank deeper and deeper into the sensory experience and was less inter-ested in the end product. It was interesting to see how Yael helped Eden complete the experience, get organized, clean herself up, and connect back to real life.

References

Solan, R. (1991). "Jointness" as integration of merging and separateness in object relations and narcissism. *The Psychoanalytic Study of the Child, 46*, 337–352.

Plate 1 Jonathan and Karen in an exercise in nine squares

Plate 2 Nechama and Limor draw animals in the forest together

Plate 3 Yael and Nofar splashing paint with syringes together

Plate 4 Yoav and Yarden create colored shapes on a black background

Plate 5 Asaf and Tamar connect the circles on the cardboard

Plate 6 Efrat and Mor draw together using warm and cool colors

Plate 7 Ya'ara and Shai work together on thirds of the page

Plate 8 Maha and Suheir following the outline of Suheir's body

Index

abandonment 68
abuse 8
Adlerian approach 17
aggression 41–42, 45, 67, 70, 71
aloneness 97, 101, 117; *see also* private/
  personal space
ambivalence 40, 66
American Art Therapy Association
  (AATA) 8
anger 41
anxiety 8, 27, 68; animals in the forest
  90; parental 28; reducing 38, 39, 45;
  therapist's 60
anxious attachment 66
art materials 9, 10, 33–34, 36; difficulties
  with 59; from a half to a whole drawing
  120; joint painting 40–41; stages
  of therapy 38–39, 45; therapy room
  32–33, 36
art therapy 8–9, 16; art in parent training
  54–56; definition of 8; *see also* parent-
  child art psychotherapy
assessment 18, 20, 27, 64; *see also*
  evaluation
attachment 4, 8, 17, 53, 66
attention-deficit hyperactivity disorder
  (ADHD) 26, 28, 34, 50, 53
attunement 119
Avimeir-Patt, R. 62
avoidant attachment 66

Bar-On, J. 11
Bat-Or, M. 34
behavioral traits 70
being together, time and space for 25, 39
Ben-Aaron, Miriam 5
Bion, W. 49
black background, colored shapes on a
  97–102

black, use of 65
body, following the outline of the
  124–128
Boote, J. 26
boundaries 30, 67, 136, 147
Bowlby, J. 4
boxes 33
Buck, E. T. 26, 43–44

change 3, 7–8; goal of parent-child
  psychotherapy 6; interpersonal
  interaction as a space for 10; therapeutic
  approaches 4
Chasid, S. 11
child development 3, 4, 69, 151
child psychotherapy 3, 4
children, focusing on 60
clay 39
closeness 11, 71, 97, 102; animals in the
  forest 91; the chase intervention 81;
  connect the circles on the cardboard
  104; connection between two partners
  on the page 68; contact between marks
  on the page 67; drawing the parent and
  child in sections 131; physical contact
  106–107; pictures from family life 135;
  relating to partner's images on the page
  69; warm and cool colors 115; *see also*
  togetherness
cognitive behavioral approaches 17
coherency 66
collaboration 69, 124, 132; *see also* joint
  paintings/drawings
collages 107–111, 132, 133–134, 135
colors: animals in the forest 88, 89;
  colored shapes on a black background
  97–102; drawing the parent and child
  in sections 129–130; following the
  outline of the body 126; "pictorial

phenomena" 65; splashing paint with syringes 91, 92, 95–96; squiggle intervention 87, 88; story between two drawings 121; tray and marble 142–144, 145; walking in gouache paints 149; warm and cool 111–115; working on thirds of the page 115–116, 117; working together without verbal communication 136

communication 9, 11; assessment of 27; joint paintings 70; leader and follower 78; modeling 44–45; working together without verbal 136–142; *see also* nonverbal communication

confidentiality 34

connection: connect the circles on the cardboard 102–105; connecting images 68, 99–101, 102

contact between marks on the page 67

"container" concept 49

containment 27–28, 95

control: animals in the forest 90; art materials 38–39, 41; attempts to take 69; drawing the parent and child in sections 131; leadership exercises 75; loss of 41; need for 66, 81; parent training 55; pictures from family life 135; story between two drawings 123

costumes 128

countertransference 62, 63

couple relationships 53–54

creativity 10; animals in the forest 89; connect the circles on the cardboard 104; joint collage 111; space for 26; squiggle intervention 87; warm and cool colors 113

dancing 149

Dent-Brown, K. 26

dependency 66, 67, 68, 69, 91, 97

destruction of artwork 41–42

Deutsch, Helene 61

developmental change 3

developmental psychology 17

dialogue 8; nonverbal 9, 34, 36, 81–82; playful 68–69

difficulties 18, 21, 58–63

disability 28, 70

display of artworks 34, 36

dissociation 66

divorce 60

drawing boards 32

"drawing language" 113

drives 90, 95

eclectic approaches 17

emotional development 3

emotional therapy 3–4

emotions 6–7, 11; joint observation 42; negative 65; parents 48, 52–53; projection of 32; therapists 62–63

empathy 61–62

envy 54

evaluation 9, 18, 20; *see also* assessment

exposure of artworks 34, 36

family exercises 124–135

family therapy 4, 17

fathers 30–31

finger paints 33, 39

Fonagy, P. 6–7

Freud, Anna 3

frustration 68, 83, 90

games 32, 36

Gavron, Tami 10, 55

gender identity 30

gifts 35

goals of therapy 6, 12, 18, 20; *see also* objectives

"good grandmother" function 27–28

gouache paints 33, 39, 41; animals in the forest 88, 89; connect the circles on the cardboard 103; drawing the parent and child in sections 129; exercise in nine squares 81; following the outline of the body 124, 125, 126; forest intervention 105; splashing paint with syringes 91–96; tray and marble 142–147; walking in 148–151; warm and cool colors 111–115; working on thirds of the page 115–117

grounded theory 22

guidance 52

Haifa model 5–8, 9–10, 12, 30–31

Harel, Y. 62

Hazut, Tamar 75

Hesse, Peretz 75

holding environment 32, 60

hope 50

idealization 66

identification 3, 62

images 9, 70–71; the chase intervention 79–81; colored shapes on a black background 99–101, 102; connection between two partners 68; creation of 84–94; joint collage 108–110; pictures

from family life 132–135; relating to partner's images on the page 68–69; separate space in a joint painting 67–68; squiggle intervention 84–88
imagination 9–10, 111, 132
independence 5, 52, 91, 111, 135
individual work 39, 97; connect the circles on the cardboard 102; forest intervention 105, 107; story between two drawings 120–123; transition to joint working 147; warm and cool colors 111, 113–115; working on thirds of the page 115–117; *see also* private/personal space
infant-mother relationship 4, 5, 11
intergenerational transference 8
internal representations *see* representations
internal working models 40, 53
interpersonal interaction 10, 12
interpretation 65
intersubjective psychology 3–4
interventions: animals in the forest 88–91; the chase 79–81; colored shapes on a black background 97–102; connect the circles on the cardboard 102–105; drawing the parent and child in sections 128–132; exercise in nine squares 81–83; family exercises 124–135; following the outline of the body 124–128; the forest 105–107; from a half to a whole drawing 117–120; joint collage 107–111; leader and follower 76–78; leadership exercises 75–83; movement exercises 84–94; parent training 50–56; pictures from family life 132–135; splashing paint with syringes 91–96; squiggle 84–88; story between two drawings 120–123; therapist interviews 18, 20; together and alone 97–123; tray and marble 142–148; walking in gouache paints 148–151; warm and cool colors 111–115; working on thirds of the page 115–117; working together without verbal communication 136–142
intimacy 5, 11, 67, 97, 102, 135; *see also* closeness

jealousy 54, 62
joint collages 107–111, 132, 133–134, 135
joint observation 42, 45, 51
joint paintings/drawings 39, 40–41, 45; encounters in interpersonal space

136–151; family exercises 124–135; leadership exercises 75–83; mother's perceptions 11; movement exercises 84–94; observation 51, 64–71; together and alone 97–123

Kaplan, H. 6, 52, 62
keeping artworks 34–35, 36
Klein, Melanie 3
Kramer, E. 41
Kris, E. 41

language of art 9, 51, 55, 65, 113
leadership 75–83, 131, 136
Lev-Wiezel, R. 11
listening to parents 49

magazines 107–111
Malchiodi, C. A. 51
marbles 142–148
marital counseling 53, 54
materials 9, 10, 33–34, 36; difficulties with 59; from a half to a whole drawing 120; joint painting 40–41; stages of therapy 38–39, 45; therapy room 32–33, 36
maternal representations 11
maternal sensitivity 8
mentalization 5, 6–7, 8, 27, 54–55; *see also* reflective thinking
"metaphorical insight" 55
modeling 44–45, 46
moments of meeting 43–44, 46
mother-infant relationship 4, 5, 11
motherhood and motherliness 61
movement exercises 84–94
music 103, 149

narrative art therapy 17
negative emotions 65
neglect 8
nine squares intervention 81–83
non-judgmentalism 50, 56
nonverbal communication 9, 10; exercise in nine squares 81–83; exposure of artworks 34, 36; language of art 51; working together without verbal communication 136–142

object relations 3, 4, 5, 17
objectives 24–28, 141; *see also* goals of therapy
observations 27; colored shapes on a black background 101–102; from a half

to a whole drawing 117–119; joint observation 42, 45, 51; joint paintings 64–71; parent training 51; squiggle intervention 87; working together without verbal communication 140
optimism 50
organization of joint painting on the page 65–67
other, self and 10, 27
outlines of the body 124–128

pace of therapy 59
painting styles 70
paper size 40, 87, 110
parent-child art psychotherapy 9–10, 12; difficulties 58–63; internal representations 10–11; interpersonal interaction 10; objectives of 24–28; presentation of the study 16–23; therapeutic setting 30–36; working with parents 48–56
parent-child psychotherapy: goal of 6; Haifa model 5–8, 9–10, 12, 30–31; history of 3–4
parent training 8, 18, 21, 31; difficulties 58–59; intervention techniques 50–56; introspection 26; working together without verbal communication 140
parental representations 5–6, 8
parenting style 61–63
parents, working with 48–56, 58–59
Parry, G. 26
pastels 41, 89, 117–120, 125, 129, 137
Patishi, R. 11
pencils 33, 38, 41
Perroni, Emilia 61
phenomenological approach 17, 42, 44, 64–65, 71
phenomenology of joint paintings 65–71
photographs 132–135
physical contact 79, 106–107
"pictorial phenomena" 64–65, 66, 67, 71
pictures from family life 132–135
play 8, 38–39; the chase intervention 81; exercise in nine squares 83; importance of playing together 52; space for 25–26; splashing paint with syringes 96
playfulness 10, 136; animals in the forest 90; connect the circles on the cardboard 104; exercise in nine squares 82, 83; joint paintings 68–69, 71; space for 25–26, 40; squiggle intervention 86, 87; story between two

drawings 121–123; warm and cool colors 113; working on thirds of the page 116–117
positive moments of meeting 43–44, 46
positive qualities of child 50, 56
practical guidance 52
private/personal space 97, 104, 117, 123; *see also* individual work
projections 32, 53, 87, 128
psycho-education 27, 52
psychoanalytic-relational school 5, 17
psychoanalytical approaches 17, 42, 147
psychodynamic approach 17

quality time 25, 63

Raz, A. 11
recycled materials 33–34
reflective thinking 6–7, 26–27, 42; safe therapeutic relationship 50; therapist's role 43, 45; *see also* mentalization
Regev, Dafna 11, 18
regression 41, 42, 84, 151
regressive materials 33
relational psychoanalysis 5, 17
relationships 3–4, 24, 40, 51; connect the circles on the cardboard 104; couple 53–54; drawing the parent and child in sections 131; family exercises 124; joint collage 110; parent training 55; pictures from family life 134–135; practical guidance 52; safe therapeutic relationship 50; working together without verbal communication 140, 141
representations 5–6, 9, 10–11, 12, 40; animals in the forest 91; art in parent training 55; drawing the parent and child in sections 131; intergenerational transference 8; joint paintings 71
responses, examining alternative 43, 46
rooms, therapy 31–33, 35–36

safety 50
sections, drawing in 128–132
self 10, 27
self-awareness 8
self-discovery 53, 91
self-esteem 8
self-expression 9, 10, 55
self-image 127, 128
self-inquiry 9
self-learning 101
self-psychology 17

self-regulation 8
self-representation 5, 7, 40
separation 11; connect the circles on the cardboard 104; drawing the parent and child in sections 131; need for 69; practical guidance 52; separate space in a joint painting 67–68; "third object" 39; tray and marble 147–148; working on thirds of the page 117
shapes 97–102
Shapira, G. 11
Siano, Judith 75
Snir, Sharon 64
social rejection 6–7
social skills 8, 26
space: for being together 25, 39; blurring of interpersonal boundaries 136, 147; organization of joint paintings on the page 65–67; playful 25–26, 40; therapy rooms 31–33
special needs 28
splashing paint with syringes 91–96
squiggle intervention 84–88
Stern, D. N. 27
stories: coherency 66; forest intervention 107; squiggle intervention 86, 87; story between two drawings 120–123
storing artworks 34–35, 36
structured activities 39–40, 45, 104–105
style 70
subject matter 70–71
supervision 65
symbolic reflection 10
symbolism of style 70
symbols 9
syringes, splashing paint with 91–96

technical difficulties 58–59, 63
therapeutic contract 18, 20, 33

therapeutic setting 18, 20, 30–36
therapists: ability to provide holding environment 60; envy and jealousy of 54; "good grandmother" function 27–28; parenting style of 61–63; presentation of the study 16–23; refraining from taking the place of parents 60–61; role of 8, 10, 18, 20, 38–46, 65; therapy rooms 31–32; as "third object" 39–40; women 31; working with parents 48–49, 52, 56, 58–59
therapy rooms 31–33, 35–36
"third object", therapist as 39–40
time for being together 25, 39
togetherness 25, 39, 40, 68; drawing the parent and child in sections 131; pictures from family life 135; psychoanalytic theory 147; relating to partner's images on the page 69; *see also* closeness
transference: child psychotherapy 3; "good grandmother" 27; intergenerational 8
transitional objects 35
tray and marble intervention 142–148
trees 105–107

University of Haifa 18

walking in gouache paints 148–151
warm and cool colors 111–115
warm-up exercises 76, 141
Winnicott, D. W. 84, 86
Winnicottian approach 25–26, 42
women therapists 31

Yakovson, Elizabeth 64, 66–69, 71